Socrates Meets Kierkegaard

Other Works of Peter Kreeft
from St. Augustine's Press

Philosophy 101 by Socrates
Socrates Meets Descartes
Socrates Meets Freud
Socrates Meets Hume
Socrates Meets Kant
Socrates Meets Machiavelli
Socrates Meets Marx
Socrates Meets Sartre
The Philosophy of Jesus (also in audio format)
Jesus-Shock (also in audio format)
An Ocean Full of Angels
Summa Philosophica
Socrates' Children: Ancient
Socrates' Children: Medieval
Socrates' Children: Modern
Socrates' Children: Contemporary
Socrates' Children [all four books in one]
Socrates' Children
Platonic Tradition
The Sea Within
I Surf, Therefore I Am
If Einstein Had Been a Surfer
Socratic Logic

Socrates Meets Kierkegaard

The Father of Philosophy Meets
the Father of Christian Existentialism

By Peter Kreeft

ST. AUGUSTINE'S PRESS
South Bend, Indiana

Manufactured in the United States of America

1 2 3 4 5 6   19 18 17 16 15 14

Library of Congress Cataloging in Publication Data
Kreeft, Peter.
Socrates meets Kierkegaard: the father of philosophy meets the father of Christian existentialism / Peter Kreeft.
pages cm
ISBN 978-1-58731-838-2 (pbk.)
1. Kierkegaard, Søren, 1813–1855. 2. Socrates.
3. Imaginary conversations. I. Title.
B4377.K73 2013
198'.9 – dc23   2013026619

∞ The paper used in this publication meets the minimum requirements of the American National Standard for Information Sciences Permanence of Paper for Printed Materials, ANSI Z39.481984.

ST. AUGUSTINE'S PRESS
www.staugustine.net

For Caleb Zimmerman
lover of Jesus
and therefore of Kierkegaard
and therefore for Socrates

CONTENTS

Introduction   1

1. The Meeting   10

2. The Question   17

3. Socrates' Philosophy Explained   24

4. Kierkegaard's Alternative to Socrates
   in Philosophical Terms   33

5. Kierkegaard's Alternative to Socrates
   in Religious Terms   53

6. Kierkegaard's alternative to Socrates in
   Psychological Terms   69

7. Kierkegaard's Argument for Believing
   the Christian Alternative to Socrates   88

8. The Gospel as Fairy Tale   99

9. The Gospel as Fairy Tale, Continued   120

10. The Argument: Reasons to Believe
    the "Fairy Tale"   130

11. Three Answers to Life's Central Question   138

12. The Decision: What Would Socrates Believe?   145

Concluding unscientific postscript   156

}vii{

Introduction

Emerson defined philosophy in one word: "Plato is philosophy and philosophy is Plato." Whitehead summarized the whole history of philosophy as "footnotes to Plato." Plato was the first philosopher with a complete system and the first philosopher from whom we have complete books. He was also the first to write dialogs and the first to combine the talents of a logical thinker with those of a poet, dramatist, and psychologist. That is not surprising; what is surprising is that he was also the last. For over 2000 years no one has rivaled him in combining intelligence with imagination, truth with beauty, philosophy with poetry, the objective with the subjective.

Except perhaps one: Søren Kierkegaard.

No philosopher ever had more strings to his bow than SK.* He wrote from many points of view, in many literary styles, about many topics (not all of them traditional philosophical topics). He should have written novels or plays, for he turned himself into a different character every time he wrote a new book. I know of no philosopher who has ever exceeded the quantity, quality *and* variety of SK's output in such a short time.

And out of it all shone forth the three most important qualities we want in any writing, in fact in any

---

* Whether from laziness, space economy, or ink conservation, the world has agreed to abbreviate his long name this way.

human work of art: truth, goodness, and beauty; intelligence, holiness, and charm. Who since Augustine has better combined all three? (C. S. Lewis, G. K. Chesterton, and Pascal are the only candidates I can point to.) And these three things are the three greatest things in the world, the only three things that never get boring, and that everyone desires, with the very deepest desires of the heart, in unlimited quantity.

Yet this amazing variety in SK had a tight and total unity. To the despair of his secular admirers, he explicitly identified his vocation as a kind of undercover missionary. He said that the ultimate task of every sentence he ever wrote was the exploration of "what it means to become a Christian." His many means to this single end were very varied, and constituted a kind of end-run around both deductive and inductive logic into a *seductive* logic, which he called "indirect communication." It is the strategy of the novelist or playwright: to show rather than to tell.

Out of the embarrassment of riches that SK left for us, I have deliberately selected two short chapters from one short book, for two reasons. The first is because I think if SK had been asked to select just one thing he would want all philosophers to read, this would be it. At issue is the fundamental step from philosophy to religion, and SK believed that the most important step philosophical reason could take, was that step beyond itself.

The second reason is that these two chapters constitute the most profound philosophical comparison I have ever read between the two most important men who ever lived, Socrates and Jesus.

I wrote another book, a few millennia ago, called *Socrates Meets Jesus*, but the title was misleading.

Physically, Socrates met only some students and professors at Have It Divinity School, who were on the way either to or from Christianity. Nobody can write fiction about Jesus Himself that is not embarrassingly silly. The figure of the Gospels simply dwarfs the greatest human imagination. And that, in the last analysis, is precisely SK's argument for believing him. (It is the argument at the end of both of these two chapters.) In the book you are now reading, Socrates meets not Jesus but Jesus's philosophical missionary, SK, who was also the one philosopher who explicitly modeled himself on Socrates himself in order to inveigle disciples of Socrates into becoming disciples of Christ. The following little drama tests how successful he would have been with Socrates himself.

Just who is questioning whom in this dialog, is the question behind all the questions, just as it is in the gospels, when Jesus, every time anyone questions him, always turns the situation around somehow so that the questioner is the one questioned. It is exactly what His Father always did whenever He appeared in the Old Testament (e.g., the burning bush dialog in Exodus 3). Like Father, like Son.

In these two chapters SK performs the imaginative "thought experiment" of casting Christianity into the two most important pagan thought-forms familiar to Socrates: philosophy and mythology. SK knows very well that Christianity is neither a philosophy nor a myth. But these are the two disarming "covers" for his mission. Instead of preaching, he philosophizes and mythologizes, he reasons and story-tells. Both are exercises in creative imagination, fantasies, thought-experiments, "what-if's."

This book does not try to summarize all of SK's

main themes. The reader needs to know only two of them, to appreciate the two chapters of his *Philosophical Fragments* that are explored here.

The first is that all of it is about "subjectivity,"or subject-hood, or self-hood, or I-ness, or personhood, that new category brought into prominence by all the "existentialists," however great their differences.

The second is that the fundamental structural outline of all of SK's work is the classification of human existence under three possible "stages on life's way" or "points of view" (perspectives), namely (1) the "aesthetic," whose fundamental categories are psychic pleasure and pain, the interesting and the boring; (2) the "ethical," whose fundamental categories are rational good and evil, right and wrong; and (3) the "religious," whose fundamental categories are faith and sin, the two possible relationships to God, positive and negative.

SK's "point of view" or "stage on life's way" in this book is halfway between the philosophical-ethical-rational-secular and the religious. To signify this, he signs this book not "Søren Kierkegaard" but "Johannes Climacus" (John the Climber, a medieval mystical figure) because he pictures himself (or the imagined author of this book) as climbing from the second of his "three stages" to the third, from the "ethical" (and rational and philosophical) to the religious. But he also adds: "Responsible for Publication: Søren Kierkegaard," to signify that he himself stands in the religious stage addressing and judging the ethical-rational-philosophical as an object rather than vice versa, even though in the text of the book he seems to do the exact opposite: he seems to take the point of view of the outside inquirer into Christianity, the point of view of the rational philosopher (in the first chapter) or the imaginative myth-maker (in the second). It is an irony similar to the one Jesus typically entered into in the Gospels: the one who is apparently questioned (Jesus) is really the questioner. That is also the irony in the dialogs of Socrates, who teaches role reversal: by assuming the role of the questioning student.

But SK tells us in his Preface *not* to ask the question he foresaw all subsequent scholars would ask about this book, viz. to what extent does it reflect SK's own point of view, but to ask the only important question, what is *true?* "**But what is my personal opinion of the matters herein discussed? I could wish that no one would ask me this question; for next to knowing whether I have any opinion or not, nothing could very well be of less importance to another than the knowledge of what that opinion might be.**" He has to trick us out of our self-trickery by which we avoid the question God is actually posing to us at the present moment—"Do *you* believe this is true?"—and by which we divert our passion to the impersonal scholarly question "Did *SK* believe it?" Very tricky, he is. Like Jesus.

Philosophy and religion have been mankind's two most ambitious undertakings, and the most interesting—if by "philosophy" is meant what the Greeks meant by it, viz. the love of wisdom, rather than what many moderns mean by it, viz. the cultivation of cleverness. SK's *Philosophical Fragments* is about the relation between these two things, between philosophy and religion, between reason and faith, between Socrates and Jesus, and about the unbridgeable gap between the two; and about the infinite existential priority of the second.

The essential claim of Christianity SK calls "the absolute paradox," which is Christ Himself, God-become-man, eternity-become-temporal, that-which-has-no-beginning becoming that-which-had-a-beginning. A paradox is an apparent contradiction, an apparent impossibility. SK was not so muddleheaded as to believe that it was a real contradiction, for that is a literally meaningless concept. Only falsehood, not truth, can contradict truth. But he did believe that this paradox forever remained opaque and mysterious to man, and could never be explained or made transparent to human reason, as most other paradoxes can.

The Church Fathers believed the same thing: they called it a "mystery." And when later Latin Christians translated the Greek word *mysterion* as *dogma*, they did not mean what "dogma" connotes to the modern mind, either something like an unarguable axiom in geometry or a dictate from a political dictator. They meant exactly what the Fathers meant: a mystery, whose inner light always shines both out of and into a darkness. However much we explore this mystery, however much we expand the light (which is what SK himself does in this book), the darkness always expands with it. If human reason, and philosophy, is to be the *ancilla theologiae,* the handmaid and servant of divinely revealed theology, and not usurp it, its primary object must always remain beyond its capacity. Its last word about itself must be the word Aquinas used to describe his *Summa*: "straw." God always speaks "out of the whirlwind," as He spoke to Job, or out of the two pillars by which He appeared to Israel in Egypt: the dark pillar of cloud and the blinding pillar of fire.

Yet philosophy remains the second greatest thing in the world; and Socrates remains, in SK's opinion, the very greatest of all philosophers; and "between man and man the Socratic relationship is the highest." Aquinas had the same opinion of Socrates (ST III, 42, 4).

Religion is higher than philosophy because God does more than any man can do. Man can *lead* us to truth, but God *brings* us truth, *gives* us truth, because He gives us Himself, and God IS truth, and you can't give what you don't have. That is SK's essential point in this book, in the simplest possible terms.

SK explicitly says in his preface that **"The present offering . . . does not make the slightest pretension to share in the philosophical movement of the day."** Yet the central question in the philosophy of religion that this book addresses was being addressed, and answered wrongly, by all the influential philosophers of SK's day; so this book *does* impact "the philosophical movement of the day." And since the issue, and the sides, are the same today as they were in SK's day, this book very much impacts today, as it impacted the generations between SK and today, e.g., by inspiring Karl Barth's "neo-orthodoxy" in reaction to the Modernism or Liberal theology represented by SK's opponents, especially Kant, Schleiermacher, and Hegel.

In 1793 Kant, in *Religion within the Limits of Pure Reason,* reduced the Gospel to a historically relative temporal expression of what he thought of as the essence of religion, viz. the timeless principles of rational morality. The historical truths of the Incarnation, Atonement, and Resurrection are not essential, then, and are lowered to what Kant calls "dogmatic" and cultic religion. SK takes exactly the opposite position: that the ultimate truth is precisely the historical Christ, eternal-truth-*in-time*, and all of our philosophical rational and ethical principles must bow before Christ, not vice versa.

Schleiermacher reduced religion not to reason, as Kant did, but to feeling. But for him also, the historical events in the Gospels are not essential, because religious feeling, or God-consciousness, is to be found in all men by nature, so that, as with Kant, no supernatural irruption or interruption is needed. Christ only had more of this religious feeling, and more perfectly, than we do, exactly as in Buddhism all men are already-enlightened Buddhas but Gotama the Buddha ("the man who woke up") was the one who realized this awakened-consciousness more perfectly than anyone else.

This brings us to Hegel, who in SK's day was to philosophy what Babe Ruth was to baseball in 1927. For Hegel, Christianity was merely an imperfect form of true philosophy (Hegel's philosophy, of course): imperfect because less abstract and conceptual. So no *historical* revelation could ever bring anything absolutely new.

All three of these philosophers really go back to Plato and his theory of "recollection": that all men by nature possess the highest truth, but have "forgotten" it. For Plato the way to "re-collect" or remember it is the Socratic method. For Kant it is moral conscience. For Schleiermacher it is religious feeling. For Hegel it is the conceptual dialectic of his System. For all of them it is—and this is the simplest way to state the essential issue—Naturalism versus SK's Supernaturalism. The very last thing any of these "Enlightenment" thinkers would allow is a miracle. "No miracles allowed here!" was the inscription on the contraceptive they put on God, or on mankind (really "womankind") to prevent us from getting pregnant with any supernatural life. In this book SK simply asks the question: what if there are cracks in this contraceptive?

(Socrates, however, not only allowed for miracles but actually lived an ongoing miracle in his unquestioned faith in the "divine voice" which directed him down surprising, unpredictable, and ultimately fatal roads—as It did to Christ.)

1.
The Meeting

KIERKEGAARD: I knew it! I knew it would happen that way—the moment I withdrew the last check from the bank—the very last cent of my inheritance from my father—I died.

Just like the grandfather clock which "stopped short, never to go again when the old man died." I am like that clock, and the money was like the old man. It was my "old man's" money, after all! Well, I am not at all surprised to find that God has a perfect sense of irony.

However, I *am* surprised at my surroundings. Surely this is not quite bright enough for Heaven, nor gloomy enough for Hell.

SOCRATES: "Not bright enough for Heaven nor gloomy enough for Hell"—that's not a bad description of your own writings, you know, O melancholy Dane.

KIERKEGAARD: You know me, Sir? Then—is this Heaven indeed?

SOCRATES: The beginning of it. You would call it Purgatory if you were a Catholic. But you didn't have enough time to finish that journey on earth, though you were beginning to move in that direction through your love of their saints and monks and mystics.

KIERKEGAARD: If you are from Heaven, Sir, why do you look more like a deformed frog than an angel? Everyone in Heaven should be beautiful, but you are the ugliest man I have ever seen.

SOCRATES: "It takes one to know one," as they say. You hardly cut a dashing figure in Copenhagen yourself. You looked like Ichabod Crane with a hunchback, something from a Charles Addams cartoon. Old women warned their children and grandchildren about you.

KIERKEGAARD: Granted, I lacked beauty. But Heaven does not. So how can *you* be a messenger from Heaven?

SOCRATES: Because beauty—or rather the ability to see it—is in the eye of the beholder.

KIERKEGAARD: How should I see you, then?

SOCRATES: As I see myself.

KIERKEGAARD: And how is that?

SOCRATES: I see my ugliness as a kind of beauty: the beauty of a perfect joke. A dark soul in a body full of light would be no joke. For an ugly soul in a beautiful body would make even its body ugly, to eyes that truly see. But what about a beautiful soul in an ugly body? The perfect irony for a philosopher. If God had given me a handsome body, like Plato's or Aristotle's, I would have been just another philosopher. As it is, I am His walking joke. A great privilege, it is, to be His walking joke. But to appreciate any joke you have to have the right sense of humor, of course. I had rather hoped that you would qualify on that score.

KIERKEGAARD: Why?

SOCRATES: For three reasons. First, you wrote more truly witty lines than any philosopher in history. Second, I thought you would understand me, since you rather idealized me when you wrote of me on earth. Third, I thought I had infected you with a little bit of my irony. You did write some profound things about irony.

KIERKEGAARD: Socrates! It is you indeed, then? In the flesh?

SOCRATES: "Flesh," you say? Hmm . . . that term clearly needs to be defined. But that is not my task today. I am here not to do my own thing, as they say, but to fulfill a task assigned to both of us by higher and wiser Authorities. We are here to discuss one of your books—in fact, the one that is most directly about me, your *Philosophical Fragments*. You are to endure one of my cross-examinations.

KIERKEGAARD: Then this cannot be Purgatory, for such a cross-examination would be pure pleasure to me.

SOCRATES: We shall see, we shall see. Perhaps both of those propositions are half-truths.

KIERKEGAARD: What do you mean?

SOCRATES: Perhaps this is Purgatory as well as Heaven, and perhaps Purgatory is the pure pleasure of finally discovering the truth as well as the pain of abject humiliation in its light.

KIERKEGAARD: My greatest pleasure will be to pursue the truth wherever it may be found, no matter how much pain and humiliation it may cause me, just as that was *your* greatest pleasure on earth, I think. I am ready to be refuted. I wrote once, you know, that every sentence I have ever written may well turn out to be wrong, except one: that God is love.

SOCRATES: That was the wisest sentence you ever wrote. But for that sentence. . . . But I am reminded of a similar sentence you once wrote about Hegel: that had he only added one single sentence to his voluminous philosophical works, he may have been justly regarded as the greatest thinker of all time, but because of the lack of that sentence he could only be regarded as a comic figure and a fool. The sentence was . . .

KIERKEGAARD: I remember: "Everything I have ever written is only a joke."

SOCRATES: That was a beautiful combination of the serious and the humorous. I could hardly have done better myself. I am tempted to plagiarize it, but the author of this book, a philosophy professor on earth, already plagiarized it in making me utter it about another thinker whom I have just cross-examined, an absurd man named Freud.*

KIERKEGAARD: Are we both merely characters in someone else's book?

SOCRATES: Yes, but the author is not merely that philosophy professor. The author is God. He assigns to each of us his proper task and his proper degree of reality.

KIERKEGAARD: Shouldn't we get on with our assignment then?

SOCRATES: Indeed we should.

* See *Socrates Meets Freud*, (St. Augustine's Press, 2014).

KIERKEGAARD: And is your assignment to converse with me, or to cross-examine me?

SOCRATES: Both. But the method is not as important as the purpose it serves. I am here for the same purpose as you are. I am not so much your interrogator, or even your teacher, as your fellow learner. We both serve the same master, Truth.

KIERKEGAARD: I wonder about our roles in this dialog. Who is teaching whom? You see, I wonder about that famous humility of yours, your claim to be always a learner and never a teacher. Was that serious or ironic?

SOCRATES: You are to interpret *that* seriously—as seriously as anything I ever said.

KIERKEGAARD: But it was your supreme irony!

SOCRATES: Yes. And *that* is what you must interpret seriously.

KIERKEGAARD: How ironic!

SOCRATES: We understand each other, then.

KIERKEGAARD: Do we also teach each other?

SOCRATES: Nothing is more likely. For in a real dialog *both* parties always learn, if only they both love truth more than victory. If a dialog leaves either party untouched, unchanged, then it is not really a dialog at all.

KIERKEGAARD: So this could be for both of us a good Purgatory and a preparation for Heaven?

SOCRATES: Yes.

KIERKEGAARD: I thought you came *from* Heaven. How can you also be *preparing* for it?

SOCRATES: There are many degrees of Heaven. Both of us may be destined to move up a notch or two. In fact, isn't that the whole purpose of everything in life?

KIERKEGAARD: I believe it is.

SOCRATES: So are you ready to begin?

KIERKEGAARD: With all my heart.

SOCRATES: I am glad to hear you say that, since we must use both the eyes of the head and the eyes of the heart to read what you have written. And that is because you used both sets of eyes to write it.

KIERKEGAARD: Which "it" are you referring to?

SOCRATES: That little book that has just appeared in our hands, your *Philosophical Fragments*.

KIERKEGAARD: Why there it is, as soon as you spoke its title! How differently things happen here—and how right and natural it seems. Also the choice of titles. A good choice for beginners, and exactly what I would have chosen if I were in charge here.

SOCRATES: That is precisely why it has been chosen. In a sense you *are* in charge here.

KIERKEGAARD: How can that be?

SOCRATES: It is with the strength of your freedom that you forge the links in the chain of your fate. The links in that chain are not made of iron; they are made of choices.

KIERKEGAARD: Am I not here for *judgment*?

SOCRATES: You are. But when you appear before the throne, you will see not only Him but also yourself

}15{

sitting on it. That is why you will be unable to escape, or even to argue.

KIERKEGAARD: And it is to prepare for that that we converse here now?

SOCRATES: It is to prepare for that that you do everything you do.

KIERKEGAARD: How wise in the ways of Heaven you seem to be, Socrates! Yet you say you too are being prepared for it.

SOCRATES: There is no contradiction between those two things.

KIERKEGAARD: So perhaps we are each other's Purgatory. Perhaps as your writings challenged and enriched mine, mine can challenge and enrich yours. What a privilege to be a Socrates to Socrates!

When my book appeared in my hand, the idea also appeared in my mind that I should read to you from it, and await your reaction and your questions.

SOCRATES: That is indeed our assignment.

KIERKEGAARD: So where shall we begin?

SOCRATES: I should like to make a radical proposal in answer to that question: that we begin at the beginning.

2.
The Question

KIERKEGAARD: Here is my beginning: **How far does the Truth admit of being learned? With this question let us begin.**

SOCRATES: What did you mean by that question? Could you "unpack" it a bit for me? I am especially curious about why you capitalized the word "Truth."

KIERKEGAARD: The philosophers distinguish two kinds of truth, as I'm sure you know: the truths of fact, or history, or events—truths that change with the passing of time, like "Caesar is dead" or "Caesar crossed the Rubicon"—and truths that are timeless, like the Platonic Forms, truths like "Justice is a virtue" or "2+2=4." Kant called them a posteriori and a priori truths: truths known only posterior to experience and truths known prior to all experience. Some call them empirical truths and rational truths, or temporal truths and eternal truths. And it was the second kind that you were always in search of, isn't that true?

SOCRATES: Yes indeed. And since you capitalize the word, I assume that you mean the higher kind of truth, the kind I was always searching for, eternal truths rather than temporal truths, what the history of philosophy would come to call Platonic Ideas or Platonic Forms.

Each of my dialogs was a search for one of these: What is Justice? or What is Piety? or What is Friendship? or What is Love? I assume that this is what you are exploring in your book.

KIERKEGAARD: Why do you assume that?

SOCRATES: Because that would make your quest a religious one, since religion is always about the eternal, and you were always exploring questions of religion in some way, however indirect. That is what you said in one of your last books, *The Point of View for my Work as an Author,* where you said this was true even of your so-called "aesthetic" works like "the Diary of the Seducer," since these apparently non-religious works set up the two essential contrasts in your philosophy: the contrast between "the aesthetic" and "the ethical" "stages on life's way" that you focused on in your first major book, *Either/Or,* and the contrast between "the ethical" and "the religious" that you focused on in works like *Fear and Trembling.*

Am I correct in this assumption?

KIERKEGAARD: You are correct—and yet you are not correct.

SOCRATES: I see you love to play riddling games.

KIERKEGAARD: As you did, Socrates. In fact you were my model. I hoped to be the Christian Socrates.

SOCRATES: But you are now no longer in the world of games, the world of shadows and hints and guesses. You are now in the world of light. Once, we both lived in the world of questions; now we are in the world of answers.

KIERKEGAARD: I see. But I also see that we are still humans, and therefore our path to those answers must remain the path of questioning, even if the path is no longer a crooked, dark, and dangerous one. Is this not so?

SOCRATES: It is indeed. That is why I was the first one sent to you by the will of Heaven, to prepare you, gradually, for the Sudden Vision that still remains afar off.

KIERKEGAARD: So I assume we may still speak in riddles, if that is the best way to approach the Light.

SOCRATES: Your assumption is correct. But I must ask again, is *my* assumption correct as I said before?

KIERKEGAARD: Which assumption?

SOCRATES: That when you speak of "Truth" in this book you are asking a religious question.

KIERKEGAARD: Yes. That is correct.

SOCRATES: And that religion always deals in some way with the eternal.

KIERKEGAARD: In some way, yes.

SOCRATES: And therefore that you were dealing with eternal Truth here.

KIERKEGAARD: I was. But I think you are making another assumption that is *not* true, and I must disabuse you of it. In fact, *two* false assumptions.

One is the assumption that my book, and my question, is about religion in general rather than Christianity in particular, or the assumption that Christianity in particular follows the same essential paths, or seeks the same kind of truth, as other religions. That is *not* my assumption, and I do not believe it is a true one.

The other is the assumption that these two kinds of truth, the eternal and the temporal, must always be separate. I do not believe that is true either.

You could even say that the questioning of these two assumptions is precisely the main point of my whole book.

SOCRATES: I am surprised to hear that. I am also confused.

KIERKEGAARD: I will try unconfuse you.

SOCRATES: How?

KIERKEGAARD: By pointing to the *connection* between these two assumptions. Do you see it?

SOCRATES: Let me think . . . I think so. Your first point is that Christianity is *not* like other religions that seek only eternal truth, and your second point is that even though it is a religion and all religion seeks the eternal, Christianity identifies the eternal with the temporal rather than separating them. Is that correct so far?

KIERKEGAARD: Yes.

SOCRATES: And the reason for both is this central claim of Christianity, about Christ—what you call the "Incarnation"—that this man is God in the flesh, the eternal Truth become a temporal man.

KIERKEGAARD: Exactly. The riddle is solved. The cat is out of the bag. So soon! Usually you take many pages to come to your main point, Socrates. Well, I suppose we are finished already, since the secret of my book is no longer a secret, and the main point has been clearly revealed. May I go now? And if so, could you kindly point me to the shortest road to what you called The Sudden Light?

SOCRATES: You are still playing games with me, Søren. You know very well that we have not finished, but only barely begun. I think nothing would surprise you more than my saying Yes to your last question.

KIERKEGAARD: You know me very well, Socrates.

SOCRATES: And vice versa.

KIERKEGAARD: I see that we can still play games with each other in this world.

SOCRATES: Yes, but we cannot lie to each other. The games here all come from and lead to the light, never the darkness. You played many such games of light in your writing career on earth, adopting many different points of view, like a novelist. So let us get on with our investigation of the game you played in this book. In comparing me with Christ, and my teaching with his, you adopted my point of view rather than his in this book, in facing the question of how we are to come to the Truth—isn't that right?

KIERKEGAARD: Yes. And since I must be totally honest here, I must tell you something else, something that you have not asked. We distinguished two kinds of truth, the temporal facts and the eternal principles, but there is a third kind of Truth that you do not know, and *that* is the real subject of this book.

SOCRATES: Oh. That puts quite a different slant on everything. And what is this third kind of truth?

KIERKEGAARD: I cannot tell it as well as I can show it. The best way to discover it is simply to follow the plot of my argument, as if it were the plot of a novel, and see where it leads.

SOCRATES: Let us do that then, by all means.

KIERKEGAARD: You did something very similar, I think, Socrates, in your dialogs: you followed an argument as if you were a detective and it was a suspect in a murder case, or long-lost lover. You philosophized *dramatically*. And so did I, largely because of your inspiration. You followed the argument wherever it went, like a rafter on a river.

SOCRATES: True, but this had two purposes: to follow the argument to the eternal truth at its end and also to follow the soul of the other person, to lead him to that end. It was not just abstract truth I was after, for my own sake, to satisfy my purely theoretical curiosity. The ultimate purpose of all my lived dialogs was the salvation of souls from ignorance and folly and vice. I tried to lead them to healing wisdom as one would lead an animal to water that was dying of thirst.

KIERKEGAARD: And that was precisely my own higher purpose too in philosophizing. It was not merely scholarship or science; it was therapy, and liberation, and transformation. I had to hide that intention, to avoid offending my patient before I could heal him. That is why I adopted his points of view rather than my own most of the time.

SOCRATES: Exactly my strategy!

KIERKEGAARD: And that is perhaps the deepest kinship between us. And yet, if we follow the argument in this book of mine, I think we will find that even there, where we seem to meet at the very heart of our vocations, to lead men to salvation, we most strikingly differ. And that difference is precisely the point of this book.

SOCRATES: I cannot wait to discover it. Let us step onto our boat and follow the river of your book together, then.

3.
Socrates' Philosophy Explained

KIERKEGAARD: I begin with what seems to be exactly your major question, rather than with anything that seems "strikingly different." I write: **How far does the Truth admit of being learned? With this question let us begin. It was a Socratic question, or became such in consequence of the parallel question with respect to virtue, since virtue was again determined as insight,** or identified with wisdom. I then mention four of your dialogs that teach this equation of virtue with knowledge: *Protagoras, Gorgias, Meno,* and *Euthydemus.*

SOCRATES: This was one of my favorite teachings: that virtue is to be equated with knowledge (or, more exactly, wisdom) and vice with ignorance (or, more exactly, folly); that all wrongdoing is caused by this ignorance—not ignorance of fact but of value, ignorance of the true good; ignorance of the great truth that only virtue can give us what we all always desire, namely happiness, true happiness, our own true good. Only because the thief does not know himself and thinks he is a bank account rather than a soul, does he steal money, for though the money fills his bank account, it empties his soul. If he only knew that the only way to the happiness he seeks is the virtue he scorns, if he only believed my equation, he would love virtue as he loves happiness, for he would identify the two. From what you write here, I cannot tell whether you agree with that teaching of mine or not. I suspect that you do not, for it sounds "rationalistic" and you are often labeled as an "existentialist" and an "anti-rationalist."

KIERKEGAARD: Both of those categories are oversimplifications. But it doesn't matter. That is not the point of this book—whether or not virtue is knowledge. It is only an explanation of why the question of Truth was so important for you: because Truth was not just theoretical but practical, not just knowledge but virtue.

SOCRATES: Let us then get on with what *is* the point of your book.

KIERKEGAARD: I next say that **In so far as the Truth is conceived as something to be learned, its non-existence (in the learner) is evidently presupposed, so that in proposing to learn it one makes it the object of an inquiry.**

SOCRATES: Indeed. For one does not seek what one already possesses.

KIERKEGAARD: And this brings up Meno's famous dilemma: **Here we are confronted with the difficulty to which Socrates calls attention in the *Meno* (80, near the end), and there characterizes as a "pugnacious proposition" [a troublesome dilemma]: one cannot seek for what he [already] knows, and it seems equally impossible for him to seek for what he does not know. For what a man knows, he cannot seek, since he [already] knows it; and what he does not know, he cannot seek since he does not know *for what* to seek.**

SOCRATES: How does you understand the second horn of my dilemma?

KIERKEGAARD: It is something like this: If we seek a lost physical object, like a lost sheep, we recognize it when we find it only because we preserve a memory image of it in our mind, which is our standard; and when we find a sheep that matches that image, we say "Aha! There is my lost sheep." We have an "Aha!" experience. There is no mystery to it. But when we seek for a lost *idea* or a lost *truth*, we seek for that standard itself. But what is the standard for recognizing the standard? Suppose, for instance, we seek the true idea of justice. We read many philosophers, and we say of each one, "No, that is not true justice." Then we read another one—Plato, let's say—and we say "Aha! Now *that* is true justice. That is what I was looking for." How do we do that?

That was your question. What is the cause and explanation for the "Aha!" experience when it comes to Truth?

SOCRATES: You understand my question very well.

KIERKEGAARD: And I think I also understand your answer to it, which I summarize this way:

Socrates thinks the difficulty through in the doctrine of Recollection (literally, recognizing, re-cognizing, cognizing-again, or remembering), **by which all learning and inquiry is interpreted as a kind of remembering: one who is ignorant needs only a reminder to help him come to himself in the consciousness of what he knows.**

"To come *to himself*," not to you, Socrates, as if you were an authority figure who *told* him the Truth. He knows it already, but he does not know that he knows it. He knows it unconsciously, not consciously, and you only raise it to consciousness. You play the part of the intellectual psychoanalyst, merely prodding us, with your questions, so that we dig and discover what was always within us. **Thus the Truth is not introduced into the individual from without** (as empirical truths are, through the senses), **but was within him.**

SOCRATES: I couldn't have put it better myself.

KIERKEGAARD: In fact, you *did!* You put it better not merely in your words but in your actions, in your life. That is my next point:

In light of this idea it becomes apparent with what wonderful consistency Socrates remained true to himself, through his manner of life giving artistic expression to what he had understood. He entered into the role of midwife (a kind of intellectual obstetrician) **not because his thought "had no positive content"**—such is the criticism commonly passed upon Socrates in our age, which boasts of its positivity much as if a polytheist were to speak with scorn of the negativity of a monotheist, for the polytheist has many gods, the monotheist only one. So our philosophers have many thoughts, all valid to a certain extent; Socrates had only one, which was absolute.

You were our intellectual midwife for a high and holy reason: **because he perceived that this relation is the highest that one human being can sustain to another.** As St. Thomas Aquinas said, "the greatest deed of charity one man can do for another is to lead him to the truth."

SOCRATES: You explain this philosophy of mine very well. But you do it only to contrast it with your Christian alternative, according to which the teacher is God Himself, and thus you drop me and my philosophy down a notch—an infinite notch, in fact. You are setting me up only to later knock me down.

KIERKEGAARD: Not so, not so! Look at what I say next: **And in this surely Socrates was everlastingly right; for even if a divine point of departure is ever given, between man and man this is the true relationship.**

SOCRATES: Well, thank you for that compliment, anyway. You seem to forget, however, that my point of departure was divine as well. Though I never claimed to be the God, I claimed to be a kind of prophet of the God. In my "Apology," every time I mentioned my vocation to philosophize, the thing that cost me my life, I mentioned its source, which was not myself and my curiosity but the God and his commandment. And remember that whenever I spoke of the God seriously I always used the singular; whenever I wanted to be ironic or comic, I used the plural.

KIERKEGAARD: I did not forget it. In fact that was the very next thing I said: **Socrates was a midwife subjected to examination by the God; his work was in fulfillment of a divine mission (Plato's *Apology*); it was in accordance with a divine principle, as Socrates also understood it, that he was by the God forbidden to beget (*Theaetetus* 150); for between man and man the maieutic (midwifing) relationship is the highest, and begetting belongs to God alone.**

SOCRATES: Yes. A midwife does not beget the baby, only helps to bring it to birth. It is the husband who begets. If Truth is the baby, I was never a husband, only a midwife. Only God is the husband of Truth. I affirm that radical difference, I do not deny it. So I do not see why you intend to *contrast* your Christian notion of how truth is learned with mine.

KIERKEGAARD: We should wait until I come to that part of the book. Be patient with me. First we have to finish expounding *your* philosophy.

SOCRATES: I will be patient. What comes next?

KIERKEGAARD: What I call "the point of departure in time," or "the Moment," the moment when the truth is learned. For you, this moment is not like the moment when a woman is impregnated and a child is conceived—a new reality—but like the waking up from a dream to realize, or recognize, the truth we already knew but forgot when we slept in ignorance. It is a new *knowledge* but not a new *reality*.

So in your view the humble insignificance of the *teacher*, as midwife rather than husband, corresponds with the humble insignificance of the *moment*, or the point of departure in time. Thus I write:

From the standpoint of the Socratic thought every point of departure in time is *eo ipso* accidental, an occasion, a vanishing moment.

The teacher himself is no more than this; and if he offers himself and his instruction on any other basis, he does not give but takes away, and is not even the other's friend, much less his teacher. Herein lies the profundity of the Socratic thought. . . . He had the courage . . . in his relations with his fellow men to be merely an occasion. . . . How rare in a time like ours, when . . . almost every second person is an authority . . . (but) no human being was ever truly an authority for another.

SOCRATES: Once again, you understand me well. But I do not understand you well. For surely you also claim to be only the messenger of the God, and not an authority. We both point above, and beyond. We may differ on who the God is, but I do not see how we differ on who *we* are.

KIERKEGAARD: We don't. But Socrates, I am not contrasting Socrates with Søren Kierkegaard, I am contrasting Socrates with Jesus Christ.

SOCRATES: But even when you contrast a man with a God, both teach Truth, even if only one of the two does so with divine authority.

KIERKEGAARD: Ah, that is precisely my contrast. It is a greater contrast than you see. The nature of teaching itself, and even the nature of Truth itself, will prove to be different when we make this contrast.

SOCRATES: I do not understand how such things can be.

KIERKEGAARD: I will try to explain them to you when we get there. But we are not there yet. We are still expounding *your* philosophy. How ironic that you are the one who is impatient now, rather than your interlocutor. May I continue the exposition? We are up to the relationship between the teacher and the learner.

SOCRATES: Proceed, by all means.

KIERKEGAARD: **With this understanding of what it means to learn the Truth, the fact that I have been instructed by Socrates, or by Prodicus, or by a servant-girl, can concern me only historically. . . . Nor can it interest me otherwise than historically that Socrates' or Prodicus's doctrine was this or that; for the Truth in which I rest was within me, and came to light through**

myself, and not even Socrates could have given it to me
.... My relation to Socrates or Prodicus cannot concern
me with respect to my eternal happiness, for this is
given me retrogressively through my possession of the
Truth, which I had from the beginning without knowing it. If I imagine myself meeting Socrates or Prodicus
or the servant-girl in the next life, then here again neither of them could be more to me than an occasion,
which Socrates fearlessly expressed by saying that even
in the lower world he proposed merely to ask questions;
*for the underlying principle of all questioning is that
the one who is asked must have the Truth in himself,
and be able to acquire it by himself.* The temporal
point of departure is nothing; for as soon as I discover
that I have known the Truth from eternity without
being aware of it, the same instant this moment or occasion is hidden in the Eternal.

SOCRATES: This is how it is.

KIERKEGAARD: Do you see how it could be otherwise?

SOCRATES: Of course. It could be that truth comes
into us from without, and in time, through our senses,
and is relative to changing things. That is the lower
truth, truth that is relative to time and change and
philosophers like the Sophists denied the existence of
Truth in the higher sense. Some of them, like
Protagoras, even denied that we could know that lower
truth and said that all we could know are appearances,
which are relative not only to time but also to the individual perceiver. Protagoras said that the individual men
is the measure of all things.

KIERKEGAARD: My contrast is not between you and

SOCRATES MEETS KIERKEGAARD

the Sophists, with their lower truth. My contrast is between you and a third kind of truth.

SOCRATES: How can such a thing be? Truth is either material or spiritual, either external or internal, either visible or invisible, either temporal or eternal. There is no third possibility.

KIERKEGAARD: Let us just suppose, as a thought-experiment, that there is. Let us see whether this thought-experiment (which I call "B") is as logically consistent as your philosophy (which I call "A").

SOCRATES: It could not be true unless it is logically consistent. But just because it is logically consistent does not mean it is true.

KIERKEGAARD: I know that. Whether it is true or not, I do not discuss until the very last two paragraphs, after the thought-experiment is completely described, in all of its contrasts to your philosophy.

SOCRATES: Let us be patient then, and continue with your contrast.

4.
Kierkegaard's Alternative to Socrates in Philosophical Terms

KIERKEGAARD: I could have selected any one of the themes of your philosophy—the nature of Truth, the nature of the teacher, the relationship between the student and the teacher, the importance of the "Moment," the point of departure in time, or the effect in the learner. But I choose to deduce everything else from this one difference: that in "B," unlike in "A," the Moment is momentous—so momentous that it sees something new come into existence.

SOCRATES: That is the Sophists' philosophy: new things come from outside, from the physical world, the world of time, into our sense experience.

KIERKEGAARD: My thought-experiment is *not* the Sophists' philosophy. For I propose that this new thing is eternal Truth.

SOCRATES: That appears to be a logical self-contradiction to me: that the new is the not-new, that the eternal is not-eternal.

KIERKEGAARD: It does indeed appear so. But appearance is not necessarily the same as reality, as you well know. It may be a paradox rather than a contradiction.

A paradox is an *apparent* contradiction but not a real contradiction. Is it not possible that my thought-experiment is only a paradox rather than the meaningless self-contradiction that it appears to be?

SOCRATES: It is theoretically possible, yes. I will believe it, however, only when I see it.

KIERKEGAARD: That is almost exactly the opposite of the definition of *faith,* which is believing something *without* seeing it.

SOCRATES: I do not reject faith out of hand, but I demand reasons for it. I do not demand empirical reasons, like the Sophists, but I do demand logical reasons, logical "seeing," so I rather like the slogan "Seeing is believing."

KIERKEGAARD: That is a popular slogan but it is exactly wrong. For if you see it, you *don't* have to believe it, because you *see* it, whether physically or logically.

SOCRATES: If that is what you mean by "faith," then I am definitely not in the market for it. But proceed. Flesh out the details of your paradox, even though it is probably impossible. We may still learn something, for even a fantasy and a falsehood can be an enlightening thought-experiment.

KIERKEGAARD: Thank you for being so open-minded. Here, then, is my hypothesis:

Now if things are to be otherwise, the Moment in time must have a decisive significance, so that I will never be able to forget it either in time or eternity, because the Eternal, which hitherto did not exist, came into existence in this moment.

SOCRATES: If that's not a self-contradiction, I don't know what is. How can eternal Truth have a beginning? How can the Eternal "hitherto *not* exist" at any time at all? How can what was always in existence come into existence for the first time? It is meaningless! A meaningful set of words does not magically become meaningful simply because you say you believe it, or even that God can do it.

KIERKEGAARD: Again I must ask you to be patient. There is a proper time for fruit to fall.

SOCRATES: I will give you the benefit of the doubt. But I must confess it makes no logical sense at all to me. I suppose it has something to do with your Christian belief that the temporal man Jesus, who was born from a woman's womb in time, is also the eternal God outside of time. The event you call the "Incarnation." You say the eternal God "came into" time. But that seems to me to be a category confusion. It tries to explain the juxtaposition of eternity with time by treating time as a space, or a place, that one could come into from "outside," as one might come into a planet or a galaxy. But even in the dimension of space there is no "outside" to space itself, no space outside space.

KIERKEGAARD: Obviously, my point does indeed have something to do with the historical Incarnation, the moment when eternity entered time. But not only that. There are many such moments, as I shall try to explain when I get to the idea of a "new birth."

But my point is not to answer those philosophical questions about Christian theology. My point is that Christianity is not a *philosophy* that some brilliant or muddle-headed man invented, a set of ideas which must be juggled in a Socratic dialog or a philosophical essay. It is a catastrophic *event* that will never be fully understood. It is news, "good news." That is the meaning of "Gospel."

SOCRATES: Then why are you contrasting it with my philosophy as if it was a competing philosophical system? That is like a contest between swimmers and runners. There is no common game both sides are playing.

KIERKEGAARD: That is exactly my point, and my contrast. I am not contrasting two sides but two games; not two philosophies but philosophy and religion. It is only to be expected that Christianity would look strange when dressed in this alien dress of the philosopher's robe.

SOCRATES: But that is what you do in your "thought-experiment." In other words, your book does to Christianity what a materialistic anthropology does to man: it looks at him *as if* he is only another animal rather than a different *kind* of creature. Your reduction of Christianity to a philosophy is only a thought-experiment, and a false one.

KIERKEGAARD: It is indeed a thought-experiment, and it is a false one if it teaches that the higher thing is in fact only the lower thing. But it is not a false one if it teaches the opposite. And it can teach the opposite by a kind of "reductio ad absurdum"—by assuming the reduction and seeing that it fails to explain the data.

SOCRATES: So by putting the philosopher's robe onto Christ we can see how badly it fits.

KIERKEGAARD: Yes. Thus the false point of view can teach the true one indirectly. In terms of your parallel with the materialistic anthropology, you can best see how different man is if you assume that he is *not* fundamentally different. Then you will be surprised, as if you saw an elephant singing opera or a dog writing novels.

SOCRATES: Let's get on with your thought-experiment, then. Explain your apparently nonsensical "B" philosophy as you explained my "A," which you yourself admitted was rational and profound and "between man and man the highest relationship."

KIERKEGAARD: The hypothesis, or thought-experiment, or presupposition, of "B" is that the Moment changes everything because the Eternal now comes into time and gets a beginning. **Under this presupposition let us now proceed to consider the consequences for the problem of how far it is possible to acquire a knowledge of the Truth.** And the first difference I look at is **The Antecedent State.**

SOCRATES: Why? Why is that the one you choose?

KIERKEGAARD: I would prefer to wait until later to answer that question, when the answer will be clearer.

SOCRATES: But I am a notoriously impatient man, so I must ask one more question about this.

KIERKEGAARD: You? Notoriously impatient? I should think that beginners in philosophy would think you the opposite. They are usually impatient with your patience. You usually take a whole dialog to get to one point, if you even get to that. Many of your conclusions were only provisional rather than certain, or ironic rather than serious, or negative rather than positive. And this was part of your strategy. But the typically modern student does not understand that, and wants results immediately, like an engineer.

SOCRATES: This is true. Yet I *am* impatient, and it is a fault. Remember the passage at the end of the dialog with Thrasymachus, which Plato recorded in the "Republic"? All I proved with that long and complex logical argument was that Thrasymachus was wrong in defining justice as the interest of the one in power. I did not prove or even define what justice really was. And instead of patiently seeking *that*, I argued about the more immediately appealing and practical questions of whether justice was a virtue or a folly, and whether it always was profitable for happiness, or whether injustice sometimes was more profitable. And because of this impatience I could not finish the dialog, and Plato had to do it for me after I died, by writing nine more books of the "Republic." And what a botched and mangled job he did! For the rest of history, everyone will blame *me* for his political obsessions and for his exaltation of the totalitarianism of the philosophers, because he added his invented Socrates to my real one. If only I had been more patient. . . . But here, here! This is meant to be your Purgatory, not mine.

KIERKEGAARD: If our common Master is as tricky and as economical as I suspect He is, it could be both our Purgatories at the same time.

SOCRATES: A disconcerting possibility! But enough diversions. Back to your text. What do you do next?

KIERKEGAARD: I began with **"Now if things are to be otherwise, the Moment in time must have a decisive significance."** Next I deduce, from this difference, a half dozen or so other differences between the pagan and the Christian hypotheses, between "A" and "B."

SOCRATES: Could you have deduced the whole half dozen, including this one about the Moment, from any one other starting point? Is the Christian house so unified that any door or window would suffice to enter the whole house?

KIERKEGAARD: If Christianity is true, it is invented by God, not man, and therefore it is a real thing rather than a dream. And all real things, unlike dreams, have this unity.

SOCRATES: So the answer is yes.

KIERKEGAARD: Yes. Why does that comfort you?

SOCRATES: Because I do not understand the importance of this beginning, or even what it could possibly mean, how it is even thinkable, much less believable. How could you possibly think that "the Eternal, which hitherto did not exist, came into existence in this moment"?

KIERKEGAARD: As I said before, if you really want to understand it—the real thing—and not just the logic of the words—then you have to be patient. My writing is like your dialogs: it is a story, not an outline. It moves from point A to point C through point B, and the order is essential.

SOCRATES: I will accept your explanation in trust. Let us move though the proper steps, then.

KIERKEGAARD: I am glad to see that you practice more faith than you preach. Well, then, under my first heading, **"The Antecedent State,"** I say: **We begin with** the Socratic difficulty about seeking the Truth, which seems equally impossible whether we have it or do not have it. The Socratic thought really abolishes this disjunction, since it appears that at bottom every human being is in possession of the Truth. This was Socrates' explanation; we have seen what follows from it with respect to the Moment. Now if the latter is to have decisive significance, the seeker must be destitute of the Truth up to the very moment of his learning it. . . . He is then in a state of Error. But how is he then to be reminded, or what will it profit him to be reminded of what he has not known, and consequently cannot recall?

SOCRATES: I think I see the logic of what you say here. For if "the moment" of learning the Truth is a real change, it logically follows that the learner must begin in Error; and if the learner already has the Truth, as I believed, even if he does not yet consciously know this, then the Moment is not any real change in actually *having* the Truth, only in *knowing* that you have it. Is that correct?

KIERKEGAARD: It is.

SOCRATES: So each position, yours and mine, or "A" and "B," is consistent within itself and inconsistent with the other position.

KIERKEGAARD: Yes.

SOCRATES: So what comes next?

KIERKEGAARD: Next let us see the consequences for the Teacher if we assume "B" instead of "A"—that is, if we assume the newness of the Moment. The Teacher . . . cannot help the learner to recall that he really knows the Truth, for the learner is in a state of Error. What the

Teacher can give him occasion to remember is, that he is in Error.

SOCRATES: So the Teacher is like a prophet.

KIERKEGAARD: Yes, like a prophet. But in this consciousness the learner is excluded from the Truth even more decisively than before, when he lived in ignorance of his Error. In this manner the Teacher thrusts the learner away from him . . .

SOCRATES: As I did many times!

KIERKEGAARD: But the (Socratic) Teacher is merely an occasion. . . . For my own Error is something I can discover only by myself, since it is only when I have discovered it that it is discovered, even if the whole world knew of it before.

SOCRATES: So if the learner does not have the Truth, the Teacher cannot remind him of it. The Teacher, then, can do nothing, it seems.

KIERKEGAARD: Or else everything. If the learner is to acquire the Truth, the Teacher must bring it to him.

SOCRATES: That is precisely what I refused to do. For I was only a midwife, an intellectual obstetrician. I was not a husband to any student. I helped him get his own baby out, but I could not put the baby in.

KIERKEGAARD: And that is exactly what the Teacher must do if the learner is in Error.

SOCRATES: And that is too much for any one human being to do for another. A man may do it to a woman's body, but no one can do it to another's mind.
I see where you are going with this, Søren: the

conclusion is that if we are in error, only God can teach us. I came to a similar conclusion myself at the end of the "Meno," but only as one of three possible hypotheses. I did not commit myself to it because I could not see that it actually happens, in history. Our myths told of lustful gods impregnating human women's bodies, but never of altruistic gods impregnating men's minds.

KIERKEGAARD: There's more. **If the learner is to acquire the Truth, the Teacher must bring it to him; and not only so, but he must also give him the condition necessary for understanding it.**

SOCRATES: A strange thing to say. Why?

KIERKEGAARD: **For if the learner were in his own person the condition for understanding the Truth, he need only recall it.** As in your philosophy, Socrates.

SOCRATES: I see.

KIERKEGAARD: **But one who gives the learner not only the Truth, but also the condition for understanding it, is more than teacher. All instruction depends upon the presence, in the last analysis, of the requisite condition; if this is lacking, no teacher can do anything.**

SOCRATES: And in your hypothesis, "B," this *is* lacking. So the teacher can do nothing. So if your hypothesis B were true, the teacher would have to do something no human teacher can do: to transform the learner before he could give him the Truth.

KIERKEGAARD: **Even more than that: he would find it necessary not only to transform the learner, but to recreate him before beginning to teach him. But this is** something that no human being can do; if it is to be done, it must be done by the God himself.

SOCRATES: Stranger and stranger becomes this hypothesis the more we look into it! How can such things be?

KIERKEGAARD: A man named Nicodemus asked Jesus exactly that question once. And my answer is the same as the one He gave to him.

SOCRATES: I must ask you to not only *give* me that answer but to *explain* it, as logically as you can. I have a good nose for logic, but little aptitude for mysticism when it comes to smelling out the truth.

KIERKEGAARD: Whether it is true or not, we shall consider later. You cannot decide whether or not to buy the painting until the painter has finished painting the picture. But I accept your demand to think it through logically. And here is the logic of it:

In so far as the learner exists, he is already created, and hence God must have endowed him with the condition for understanding the truth. For otherwise his earlier existence must have been merely brutish . . .

SOCRATES: That is a valid inference. Please proceed.

KIERKEGAARD: But in so far as the Moment is to have decisive significance (and unless we assume this, we remain at the Socratic standpoint), the learner is destitute of this condition, and must therefore have been deprived of it.

SOCRATES: That logically follows. I'm glad to see you are not abandoning the law of non-contradiction for some mystical "higher consciousness." What is the next step of your argument?

KIERKEGAARD: This deprivation cannot have been due to an act of the God (which would be a contradiction), nor to an accident (for it would be a contradiction to assume that the lower could overcome the higher); it must therefore be due to himself.

SOCRATES: All very consistent. So then the learner is in the state of being at fault for losing this "condition"—whatever that is—the condition for understanding the Truth.

KIERKEGAARD: Yes.

SOCRATES: And this is the state you call "Error."

KIERKEGAARD: Yes. Error is then not only outside the Truth, but polemic in its attitude toward it; which is expressed by saying that the learner has himself forfeited the condition, and is engaged in forfeiting it. . . . But this state, the being in Error by reason of one's own guilt, what shall we call it? Let us call it *Sin*.

SOCRATES: Now you identify the intellectual term, Error, with the moral term, Sin. Is that not a confusion of categories?

KIERKEGAARD: No.

SOCRATES: It certainly seems to be. What is the relation between these two terms, then?

KIERKEGAARD: "Sin" is the deeper term. It is the ontological source of the intellectual Error.

SOCRATES: I am confused. Or, rather, you seem to me to be confused. For "Sin" means "disobeying the God." That is a moral term, not an intellectual term. Its opposite is Virtue, not Truth. "Error," on the other hand, is an intellectual term, not a moral term. Its opposite is "Knowledge," not "Virtue." "Sin" and "Sanctity" are simply the religious version of "Vice" and "Virtue." You seem to be confusing categories here.

KIERKEGAARD: I am surprised to hear *you* say that, Socrates, for it was you who taught that all vice was really only ignorance.

SOCRATES: I meant that it was *caused* only by ignorance—moral ignorance, ignorance not of facts but of values. But even when I closely connected the intellectual and the moral, as cause and effect, I distinguished these two powers of the soul. But you seem to confuse them.

KIERKEGAARD: That is because I mean to point to a deeper dualism than either the intellectual dualism between truth and error *or* the moral dualism between virtue and vice.

SOCRATES: And that is a dualism on the ontological level?

KIERKEGAARD: Yes.

SOCRATES: You spoke of "the ontological source of the intellectual Error"; what is that?

KIERKEGAARD: There are two and only two possible ontological states, states of being, in relation to God: either you are or are not in a relationship with God that could be called being born again, or being twice-born, or being saved, or being possessed of divine life, or being justified, or being sanctified, or being in a state of grace, or sanctifying grace—there are many different theological terms for the same thing. The opposite of this is the state of Sin.

SOCRATES: So Sin is a state before it is an act.

KIERKEGAARD: Yes.

SOCRATES: And the opposite of Sin, in a single word, is . . .

KIERKEGAARD: Faith. St. Paul says, "Whatever is not of faith is sin."

SOCRATES: But "faith" is an intellectual term. It means "belief." Its opposite is "unbelief" or "doubt."

KIERKEGAARD: No. Not as I use these two terms, or as the New Testament uses them. "Faith" is an ontological term, not an intellectual term. And "Sin" is an ontological term, not a moral term. And the two are opposites. Faith is the positive relationship with God and Sin is the negative relationship with God.

SOCRATES: Thank you for clarifying that. I understand how you define these terms now, and how they are related in your hypothesis "B." But that is not at all the same thing as understanding the reality they mean.

KIERKEGAARD: That is indeed a crucial distinction.

SOCRATES: I still do not understand what you mean by "the condition for understanding the Truth." But I think I see how all your other terms fit together in your overall strategy. And I would like to test my understanding with you.

KIERKEGAARD: Test away.

SOCRATES: I think you are using intellectual terms, philosophical terms, like "teacher" and "understanding" and "error" and even "truth" to make a point that is deeper than the intellectual point or even the moral point: a religious point. You are transposing your religious hypothesis into a philosophical format, the format of a thought-experiment.

KIERKEGAARD: That is exactly what I am doing.

SOCRATES: Why do you do this?

KIERKEGAARD: To relate it to your format, which is the format of the philosophers.

SOCRATES: In other words, to be a missionary to the philosophers.

KIERKEGAARD: Yes. I hope that the thought-experiment can become a step towards a deeper thing, a faith-experiment, something you not only *think* but *live*.

SOCRATES: Why is this "faith" so important for you?

KIERKEGAARD: Because it is "the condition for understanding the Truth."

SOCRATES: Apparently you mean something more by "faith" than what I meant by it, namely right opinion, right belief.

KIERKEGAARD: Yes. That is why I called it something you not only think but live.

SOCRATES: So it is right belief plus right action. But that is still just something intellectual plus something moral, but not necessarily something religious. But you mean something religious.

KIERKEGAARD: Yes.

SOCRATES: Is it something more than intellectual belief about the God, the religious object, plus moral choices that are specified by the will and law of this

God, this religious object, and motivated by the attempt to please or attain this religious object?

KIERKEGAARD: Yes. It is more than that.

SOCRATES: Then I do not understand what it is.

KIERKEGAARD: It exists in the realm of subjects, not objects—the realm of relationships between persons. It is something like spiritual marriage, or pregnancy.

SOCRATES: That is what you mean by "faith"? That "relationship" is "the condition"?

KIERKEGAARD: Yes.

SOCRATES: And you said that this "condition" was missing in us, and was missing because we ourselves had thrown it away, and that only the God could restore it, and that without it we could not possibly understand the Truth.

KIERKEGAARD: Yes.

SOCRATES: So faith is not in our power but is the gift of the God.

KIERKEGAARD: Yes.

SOCRATES: So we can do nothing about it but only wait around and hope that the gift will be given.

KIERKEGAARD: No. We can ask for it.

SOCRATES: And *then* just wait around hoping the gift will be given.

KIERKEGAARD: No, we can be certain that it will be given.

SOCRATES: Why?

KIERKEGAARD: Because it was solemnly promised by the God. "Ask and it shall be given to you, seek and you shall find, knock and the door will be opened unto you. For every one who asks, receives; every one who seeks, finds; to every one who knocks the door will be opened."

SOCRATES: Can you prove that this promise is true?

KIERKEGAARD: No. But you can believe it.

SOCRATES: So you need faith from the beginning.

KIERKEGAARD: Yes.

SOCRATES: So you have to have faith in order to receive a gift from the God, but you have to receive a gift from the God in order to have faith. It looks like a catch-22.

KIERKEGAARD: It is not a causal relationship, with one of those two things coming first and causing the other. These two things, God's act of giving it and our act of choosing it, are probably two sides, or two dimensions, of one and the same event.. They look different only from our point of view, but they're one thing from God's point of view.

SOCRATES: I do not understand that.

KIERKEGAARD: Neither do I. Because I don't have God's point of view.

SOCRATES: Than how can you believe it, if you can't understand it?

KIERKEGAARD: Can a child believe his parents?

SOCRATES: Of course.

KIERKEGAARD: But can he understand them fully?

SOCRATES: Not fully. But unless he understands *something* of them, how can he believe them?

KIERKEGAARD: He can't.

SOCRATES: And something is not nothing.

KIERKEGAARD: No. But neither is it everything.

SOCRATES: I think I still do not understand just what this "faith" of yours means, but at least I understand where it is, its address, so to speak. It's somewhere between Ignorance Avenue and Knowledge Street.

KIERKEGAARD: But it's not first of all in the city of the mind, but in another city. So it's not just "right opinion," as you said it was in the "Meno" and the "Republic."

SOCRATES: What city is it in?

KIERKEGAARD: The city of personal relationship.

SOCRATES: And you say that only if you have faith, can you understand?

KIERKEGAARD: Yes. As little children can't really understand their parents unless they trust them. Even the very rational medieval philosophers thought that. Two of their slogans were "I believe in order to understand" and "Unless you believe, you will not understand."

SOCRATES: I always believed it was the opposite: that reason came first; that if you had reason from the beginning, you might reason your way to faith and understand it.

KIERKEGAARD: That is precisely the difference between us.

SOCRATES: But in your writing this book, are you not appealing to reason? Do you not offer some kind of *argument* for believing your "hypothesis B," which is Christianity? And is that not using my strategy rather than yours, using reason as a road to faith rather than faith as a road to reason?

KIERKEGAARD: It is both. The two roads do not exclude each other, though one is higher or deeper than the other. The deeper understanding can come only through faith. But the less deep understanding, mere human reason, can also approach faith, as a road can approach the sea. But at the end of the road, if you want to swim, you cannot do it with a chariot. You can only get out of the chariot and leap the leap of faith into the sea.

SOCRATES: So this whole book, which is about the higher road, is an example of the lower road.

KIERKEGAARD: Yes.

SOCRATES: And only in the last two paragraphs do you directly invite the chariot driver to leap out of his chariot into the sea.

KIERKEGAARD: Yes.

SOCRATES: But in those last two paragraphs, don't you give a reason for this leap of faith?

KIERKEGAARD: I do. But it is not a demonstration, a certainty, an unanswerable syllogism.

SOCRATES: I see—I think. Thank you for explaining where you are taking me on this road of yours, even before we get there, even though you refused to do it earlier in our conversation. Why the change of mind, if I may ask?

KIERKEGAARD: I thought at first that it would harm your understanding to know the end of the road too soon, just as in one of your Socratic dialogs it would have harmed the understanding of the other party if he had been told where the conversation would end up *before* he was actually led there.

SOCRATES: And what made you think differently?

KIERKEGAARD: I realized that I am not Socrates and you are not the other. You are Socrates and I am the other. I must follow your questions in this conversation, rather than vice versa.

SOCRATES: Admirable humility! Only the God could elicit such a reversal. So I thank him for changing your mind and thus making it easier for me to understand you.

KIERKEGAARD: I still wonder which of us He is intending to teach in this conversation.

SOCRATES: I wonder that too. In fact I have wondered that in every conversation I have ever had.

5.
Kierkegaard's Alternative to Socrates in Religious Terms

SOCRATES: We should return to our exploration of your alternative hypothesis, your thought-experiment "B," which is the mask you put on the Christian faith. We are up to the question of the identity of the Teacher, I believe.

KIERKEGAARD: Yes. The Teacher, then, is the God, and he gives the learner the requisite condition and the Truth. What shall we call such a Teacher?—for we are surely agreed that we have already far transcended the ordinary functions of a teacher.

In so far as the learner is in Error, but in consequence of his own act (and in no other way can he possibly be in this state, as we have shown above), he might seem to be free; for to be what one is by one's own act is freedom. And yet he is in reality unfree and bound and exiled; for to be free from the Truth is to be exiled from the Truth, and to be exiled by one's own self is to be bound.

SOCRATES: O please let me interrupt you! I think I see your point now, for the first time, and I would dearly love to be tested by you to see whether or not I really see. For the truly blind are not those who do not see but those who do not even see that they do not see.

KIERKEGAARD: What do you think you see now, Socrates?

SOCRATES: That when you say "Error" you mean Sin; and when you say "Truth" you mean the God Himself; and when you say "the condition for understanding the Truth" you mean Faith; and When you say "understanding" you mean "willingly accepting." When I say these things I am doing philosophy, but when you say them you are doing religion. In your hands each of these categories has become new.

KIERKEGAARD: This is true, for it is as my Teacher said: "Behold, I make all things new." And do you see the common thread that holds all four new categories together in their newness? In other words, do you see the pervasive difference between philosophy and religion, between all things philosophical and all things religious?

SOCRATES: I think so. They are all made personal. They are made subjective. But not as the Sophists Did.

KIERKEGAARD: That is true. How do you see the difference?

SOCRATES: The Sophists made truth subjective but you made it subjectivity. When you wrote, in your *Concluding Unscientific Postscript,* that "truth is subjectivity," you did not mean what Protagoras the Sophist meant when he said that the individual man is the measure of all Things. For you the God is the measure of all things, but the God is a Person, an I, a subject, whereas for philosophy He is an object of thought. Am I on the right track? Is that indeed what you mean?

KIERKEGAARD: I could not have put it more clearly myself.

SOCRATES: But even though I see this distinction, and I see what you do not mean, I do not see what you do mean by saying that "truth is subjectivity." Elsewhere you write that "truth is an equivalent expression for faith." I do not see what this means, though I think I see what it does not mean. It does not mean what Protatoras seems to mean: that whatever you happen to believe, however silly or stupid it may be, is true for you, and is the only truth you can ever know.

KIERKEGAARD: Can you give a guess, or an approximation, to what you think I do mean?

SOCRATES: I think you mean that truth is found in three places. First it is in the God, as the true or authentic object of faith. And you say that "truth is subjectivity" here because the God is not an idea, which is only a mental object, but a subject, a person, an I. Second, that it is in the true, authentic relationship to this God which you call "faith." Third, that is is in the one who has this faith, which makes him authentic or "true."

KIERKEGAARD: You see that very clearly, Socrates. What do you not see, then?

SOCRATES: I do not see what you mean by Sin as the opposite of Faith. I do see that you are disguising your religious categories in my philosophical clothing precisely to distinguish them from philosophy, as if one were to distinguish a man from a monkey by dressing up a monkey in a man's suit and observing how he acts in human company. But I think I do not understand this concept of Sin.

KIERKEGAARD: You do indeed see what it is that you fail to see, Socrates. And since Sin is the opposite of Faith, you do not understand Faith either. And since Faith is the true relationship with the God who is true, you do not understand the God either.

SOCRATES: So I am a blind man who does not understand the concept of darkness because he has never seen the light. I do not understand Faith because I do not understand Sin as its opposite.

KIERKEGAARD: Precisely.

SOCRATES: And why do I not understand it? What do I lack?

KIERKEGAARD: You do not understand it because you pagan Greeks never had the experience of the faith-relationship with the God that His chosen people the Jews had, and their successors the Christians. You were never married to God, therefore you cannot understand the concept of a divorce from Him.

SOCRATES: And are you now trying to lead me to this thing that is unknown to me, this new relationship to the God which you call by analogy "being married to the God" by contrasting it so sharply with the things I know through my philosophy?

KIERKEGAARD: Precisely. You see my goal, and my method, and the difference between my religion and your philosophy.

SOCRATES: But I do not yet understand your religion, because I am not Kierkegaard, I am only Socrates.

KIERKEGAARD: That is true. But you do understand

that you do not understand it, precisely because you are Socrates.

SOCRATES: Therefore there is hope for me. But this hope is blocked for me by Meno's dilemma: How can I come to *recognize* this new thing if I have never before *cognized* it?

KIERKEGAARD: Excellent question!

SOCRATES: And the excellent answer is . . . ?

KIERKEGAARD: Only by the grace of the One who makes all things new.

SOCRATES: And when will this grace be given?

KIERKEGAARD: In the Moment which is your new birth.

SOCRATES: I can only echo another philosopher, then, in asking: How can an old man be born again? Can he enter into his dead mother's womb? How can such things be?

KIERKEGAARD: Because His grace gives not only the Truth, which is Himself, but also the power of personally appropriating it, which I have called "the condition for understanding it" (using the disguised categories of philosophy for it). This condition is Faith.

SOCRATES: So not only is the God Himself a grace, or a gift, but Faith is also His gift.

KIERKEGAARD: Yes.

SOCRATES: And how do I receive this gift?

KIERKEGAARD: By asking for it. For all who ask, receive; all who seek, find; the door is opened to all who knock.

SOCRATES: I have been seeking and knocking on the door of the unknown God all my life.

KIERKEGAARD: Then you will surely find Him.

SOCRATES: When?

KIERKEGAARD: When the Moment comes. And when it comes, it relativizes all other time. It cannot be defined or predicted by ordinary time. The God is not a chariot that obeys a schedule.

SOCRATES: I see the consistency of your "experiment of thought" (for that is what it is for me so far, and not an experiment in faith). I see how each part of it fits with all the others. I also see how different it is from my philosophy in each point and as a whole. But I fear I am still in the position of the blind man, as I was at the end of Book I of Plato's "Republic." I have yet to understand the Idea.

KIERKEGAARD: That is because it is not an Idea.

SOCRATES: Then I shall never understand it.

KIERKEGAARD: No man can understand it. But one can believe it.

SOCRATES: I do not understand how one can believe something he cannot understand.

KIERKEGAARD: Do you believe you exist?

SOCRATES: Of course.

KIERKEGAARD: Do you understand your existence?

SOCRATES: Of course not. That is why I philosophize.

KIERKEGAARD: Quod erat demonstrandum.

SOCRATES: But I want to know the God I seek and hope for.

KIERKEGAARD: But the God is not an Idea. The God is a Person. Knowing a Person is not the same as knowing an Idea.

SOCRATES: I do not see how the object of knowing can be anything other than an idea.

KIERKEGAARD: Then why did you famously command us to "know thyself"?

SOCRATES: Touché, Søren! Hoist on my own petard, I am. It seems I did not really know what I was saying when I said that.

KIERKEGAARD: What did you mean by it when you said it?

SOCRATES: I meant simply that you should know what you are.

KIERKEGAARD: Fine. But you are not just a "what" but also a "who."

SOCRATES: I fear that all I meant when I said "know thyself" was "know what you are saying when you speak, know the meaning of your words." And I failed to do even that myself! What an egregious error!

KIERKEGAARD: Should we not then further explore this very notion, Error? That was what the text of my book was exploring when you interrupted me with your sudden insight about your failure of insight.

SOCRATES: Oh, yes, let us return to the words of your text, by all means.

KIERKEGAARD: Back to your familiar territory of words?

SOCRATES: Yes, for the very words may help to free me from imprisonment in words.

KIERKEGAARD: I accept that noble motive. Here, then, is what I say next:

But since he is bound by himself, may he not loose his bonds and set himself free? For whatever binds me, the same should be able to set me free when it wills; and since this power is here his own self, he should be able to liberate himself.

SOCRATES: A very logical objection, and exactly the one I would have proposed.

KIERKEGAARD: **But at any rate he must will it. Suppose . . . that he wills his freedom. In that case, i.e., if by willing to be free he could by himself become free, the fact that he had been bound would become a state of the past, tracelessly vanishing in the moment of liberation; the Moment would not be charged with decisive significance.**

But that was the premise of the whole hypothesis: that the Moment *was* decisively significant—so much so that he received a new being in that Moment.

SOCRATES: I do not understand what this "new being" might mean, but I see the logic of your argument for all these beliefs in "B" once you grant one of them. It is a consistent "package deal." Please proceed.

KIERKEGAARD: I here append a long footnote, which is more important to the argument than it appears to be. I say:

Let us take plenty of time to consider the point, since there is no pressing need for haste.

SOCRATES: I must interrupt you with a sharp word of praise. This is a most auspiciously wise beginning! I strongly suspect that nearly all errors, both in philosophy and in life, begin in this mis-relationship to time, taking it as our master rather than our servant.

KIERKEGAARD: Thank you. You were my inspiration there, you know. Thus I go on:

Let us talk about this a little in the Greek manner. Suppose a child had been presented with a little sum of money and could buy with it either a good book, for example, or a toy, both at the same price. If he buys the toy, can he then buy the book for the same money? Surely not, since the money is already spent. But perhaps he may go to the bookseller and ask him to make an exchange, letting him have the book in return for the toy. Will not the bookseller say: My dear child, your toy is not worth anything; it is true that when you still had the money you could have bought the book instead of the toy, but a toy is a peculiar kind of thing, for once it is bought it loses all value. Would not the child think that this was very strange?

And so there was also a time when man could have bought either freedom or bondage at the same price, this price being the soul's free choice and commitment in the choice. He chose bondage; but if he now comes forward with a proposal for an exchange, would not the God reply: Undoubtedly there was a time when you could have bought whichever you pleased, but bondage is a very strange sort of thing; when it is bought it has absolutely no value, although the price paid for it was originally the same. Would not such an individual think this very strange?

Again, suppose two opposing armies drawn up in the field, and that a knight arrives whom both armies invite to fight on their side; he makes his choice, is vanquished and taken prisoner. As prisoner he is brought before the victor, to whom he foolishly presumes to offer his services on the same terms as were extended to him before the battle. Would not the victor say to him: My friend, you are now my prisoner; there was indeed a time when you could have chosen differently, but now everything is changed.

Was this not strange enough? Yet if it were not so, if the moment had no decisive significance, the child must at bottom have bought the book, merely imagining in his ignorance and misunderstanding that he had bought the toy; the captive knight must really have fought on the other side, the facts having been obscured by the fog, so that at bottom he had fought on the side of the leader whose prisoner he now imagined himself to be.

In fact, that is precisely the philosophy of the Hindus and Buddhists, if I understand them aright. Eternity—Nirvana, Buddha-mind, Satori, Kensho, Mukti, Sat-cit-ananda—there are many terms for this one central thing, this eternal thing, in Eastern theology, just as there are many terms for the one central thing in Christian theology, this new thing.

And this eternal thing, eternal Truth, was the ultimate end of your philosophy too, Socrates; so you were on the Hindu-Buddhist side rather than the Christian side, though in a more logical rather than mystical way.

SOCRATES: Yes. For Truth—the Truth we speak of here—is eternal, not temporal.

KIERKEGAARD: Ah, yes. That is your hidden presupposition.

SOCRATES: No, it is neither hidden nor a presupposition. It is something we agreed about explicitly at the beginning of this conversation. And it is not a presupposition, which may be either true or false; it is simply a tautology, a correct definition of the term. I thought we had simply agreed to speak about eternal Truth, Truth with a capital T, rather than temporal truth.

KIERKEGAARD: But I also spoke of a third kind of truth, one that is both.

SOCRATES: And I did not understood that then, nor do I understand it now. "Eternal" and "temporal" logically exclude each other. What is eternal has no beginning, and what is temporal does. Eternal Truth cannot acquire a beginning in time, though our knowledge of it can.

KIERKEGAARD: And that is precisely what I would disagree with.

SOCRATES: And that is precisely what I cannot understand.

KIERKEGAARD: But you do understand this: that the logical consequence of your "A" hypothesis is that **Thus interpreted, the Moment receives no decisive significance; and yet this was the hypothesis ("B") we proposed to ourselves in the beginning (that it *did*).**

SOCRATES: And how does that affect the question of freedom that you deal with in that long footnote about the boy who wanted to exchange his toy and the soldier who wanted to change his allegiance?

KIERKEGAARD: By the terms of our hypothesis ("B"), therefore, he will not be able to set himself free . . .

SOCRATES: Why not, if he is in time and change?

KIERKEGAARD: Because he forges the chains of his bondage with the strength of his freedom.

SOCRATES: Another apparent contradiction.

KIERKEGAARD: But an easy one to explain.

SOCRATES: Only if the term "freedom" is not used univocally here.

KIERKEGAARD: That is exactly right.

SOCRATES: And what are its two different meanings?

KIERKEGAARD: The two that Augustine distinguished. The lower freedom is *liberum arbitrium*, free will or free choice. The higher one is *libertas*, liberty. The lower freedom is freedom from determinism, fate, necessity or compulsion, freedom from the external chain. The higher freedom is freedom from sin, which is slavery to the internal chain. The lower freedom is a means by which we can attain the higher one, or rather choose to accept it as a gift of divine grace. But that lower freedom is also the means by which that higher one can be refused.

SOCRATES: So it is only an apparent contradiction because the freedom with which he forges the chains of his bondage is not the same as the freedom that is the opposite of that bondage.

KIERKEGAARD: Yes. Thus He forges the chains of his (higher) bondage with the strength of his (lower) freedom, since he exists in it without compulsion;

and thus his bonds grow strong, and all his powers unite to make him the slave of sin.

SOCRATES: It is like an addiction, then, made stronger by each indulgence.

KIERKEGAARD: Yes.

SOCRATES: I think I see your point now. You are disagreeing with my view that it is only ignorance that enslaves us, that all evil comes from ignorance and is healed by knowledge, by wisdom, which comes from teaching. You are saying that an addict is not helped by someone teaching him the truth that he is an addict and that addiction is bad for him, because he already knows that, but that knowledge does not free him.

KIERKEGAARD: Yes, that is implied in what I say. But my point here is that there is another kind of Truth, and another kind of Teacher, that *can* free him, by giving him the two things a Socratic teacher cannot. Thus I say: **What shall we now call such a Teacher, one who restores the lost condition and gives the learner the Truth? Let us call him** *Savior*, **for he saves the learner from his bondage and from himself; let us call him** *Redeemer*, **for he redeems the learner from the captivity into which he had plunged himself, and no captivity is so terrible and so impossible to break as that in which the individual keeps himself** . . .

Such a Teacher the learner will never be able to forget . . .

And now the Moment. Such a moment has a peculiar character. It is brief and temporal indeed, like every moment; it is transient as all moments are; it is past, like every moment in the next moment. And yet it is decisive, and filled with the Eternal. Such a moment ought to have a distinctive name; let us call it the *Fullness of Time.*

SOCRATES: "The Fullness of Time"—I believe that was the term used by the early Christian writers, the "Church Fathers," to refer to the time which divine providence had prepared for that event you Christians call the Incarnation. It included the greatest achievements of ancient civilization, Greek language and Greek philosophy, Roman law and Roman peace, and all of these things made up a kind of road for the Christian chariot to travel on, a landing field for the heavenly bird to land on.

KIERKEGAARD: Yes.

SOCRATES: So it means the moment when the eternal God entered time, thus joining the two kinds of truth.

KIERKEGAARD: Exactly.

SOCRATES: It is this "landing" of eternity in time that I cannot wrap my mind around. And even if it did happen, what does it have to do with me, who died four hundred years earlier, or you, who were not born until nineteen hundred years later?

KIERKEGAARD: It opened up the possibility for it to happen again. The very same God who "landed" at this one time also opened up not only that one time but all times for the invasion from eternity.

SOCRATES: What kind of invasion? Will he be born again in a stable? Or will it be angels that come? What do you mean?

KIERKEGAARD: No, it is more than that. He continues to "land," as you put it, in each individual soul.

SOCRATES: You mean by each individual remembering him and believing the truths he taught and the truths his Church teaches about him? But that is no more than what *I* taught: that eternal truth can be "remembered" by anyone in time if he is taught by a good teacher.

KIERKEGAARD: No, it is more than that. He called it being "born again." It is a real change, not just a mental change. It is a microcosm of the macrocosmic Incarnation. Thus the words the angel of God spoke to Mary nineteen hundred years before my time are also spoken to every individual who opens his ears, so to speak—not just the ears of reason but the ears of faith. Remember, "faith" means more than just "belief." It means something like a woman's freely accepting a new kind of pregnancy, not from the flesh of a man into her flesh but from the Spirit of God into her spirit:

The Holy Spirit shall come upon you, and the Power of the Most High shall overshadow you; and thus that holy One to be born of you shall be called the Son of God.

It is to persuade men to accept that pregnancy in their souls that Christian missionaries work, and speak, and pray.

SOCRATES: And you are one of these missionaries? Is that your secret identity?

KIERKEGAARD: That is exactly what I said in my last complete book, *The Point of View for my Work as an Author.* And that is the book almost all my critics ignore because they are embarrassed by it. What a scandal!—that this clever philosopher, with so many original things to say, should turn out to be, in the end, nothing but a Christian missionary in disguise! How tedious! I even said explicitly in that book that every single word I had ever written, even the scandalous "Diary of the Seducer," which is an apologia for the polar opposite way of life, could not be correctly understood in any other way except as part of my missionary strategy, my disguise, my spy's cover. For I thought of my whole philosophical vocation as the call to be a missionary—not to pagans like yourself but to those who thought they were Christians simply because they had certain *opinions* or even merely because their names had been registered on the rolls of a church. My task was to smuggle Christianity back into Christendom, in disguise. It was a task which, I foresaw, would become more and more essential in my native country, and continent, and civilization.

SOCRATES: So this conversation that we are having here, now, which I thought was my philosophical task by deductive logic to induce you into reason—are you saying that this is really part of your missionary task to seduce me into faith?

KIERKEGAARD: Might it not be both?

6.
Kierkegaard's Alternative to Socrates in Psychological Terms

SOCRATES: I suppose that is possible—and if so, it would be a remarkable trick of divine providence, as well as a very economic arrangement, with one conversation serving as a means to two different ends at once.

And I suppose when we evaluate your hypothesis "B," later in this conversation—assuming we understand it enough to dare to evaluate it—we may be able to see whether your faith has educated my reason or whether my reason has educated your faith, or both.

But we must first finish painting your picture, your thought-experiment, before we can evaluate it. So what is your next point?

KIERKEGAARD: We have explored
(1) **The Antecedent State** and
(2) **The Teacher,** so now we must explore
(3) **The Disciple,** focusing on the *change* in the disciple.
When the disciple is in a state of Error (and otherwise we return to Socrates) but is none the less a human being, and now receives the condition and the Truth, he does not become a human being for the first time, since he was a man already. But he becomes another man; not in the frivolous sense of becoming another individual of the same

quality as before, but in the sense of becoming a man of a different quality, or as we may call him: *a new creature.*

SOCRATES: I cannot conceive what kind of a change this could be. It must be either an essential change or an accidental change, for those are the only two kinds of change that are logically possible. If it is merely an accidental change, then you very misleadingly exaggerate it when you call it a **"new birth"** and a **"new creature"** and say that **"the eternal, which hitherto did not exist, came into being in this moment"**—whatever that could possibly mean. So may we eliminate this possibility of a merely accidental change?

KIERKEGAARD: It is not merely an accidental change, like growing older, or wiser, or better. It is an essential change, like birth. That is why it is called a "new birth."

SOCRATES: Because at birth something **"which hitherto did not exist came into being in this moment"**?

KIERKEGAARD: Yes.

SOCRATES: And death is also an essential change, for then that which did exist no longer exists, isn't that right?

KIERKEGAARD: Yes.

SOCRATES: So we can call this change an essential change.

KIERKEGAARD: Yes. Or we might want to call it an "existential change," a change in existence, since something new comes into existence for the first time.

SOCRATES: But you just said that in this "new birth" the man does not become a human being for the first time, since he was a human being already. So he already had his essence, his humanity. So it is *not* an essential change, then.

KIERKEGAARD: It *is*.

SOCRATES: So the man receives a kind of second essence?

KIERKEGAARD: You might say that, if you insisted on your Socratic language of essences.

SOCRATES: Let me try to understand it by analogies. Is it something like this, then?—like a man eating the meat of a pig, so that the pig cells are transformed into human body cells, so that the matter in the pig could now perform actions, such as thinking rationally with a human brain, which the pig could never have performed when it was only a pig? Or like a pig eating some corn, so that the matter in the corn can now perform acts like running or uttering squeaky noises, acts that mere corn could never have performed? Or like the corn assimilating the nutrients in the earth so that these inorganic chemicals now grow, since they are now part of an organism? Is it like that?

KIERKEGAARD: As you know, Socrates, an analogy is almost always accurate in one way and inaccurate in another.

SOCRATES: So how is this analogy not accurate?

KIERKEGAARD: The inorganic chemicals are destroyed or replaced with organic chemicals when the growing corn assimilates them. Corn ceases to be corn in the stomach of the pig that eats it. And when man eats a pig, the pig ceases to be. But in the "new birth" man is not destroyed, nor does he cease to be. In fact, he is more man, not less, in the "new birth." The God perfects the man's humanity by somehow uniting it with His divinity.

SOCRATES: I understand your words but I must confess I do not understand the reality they mean to convey.

KIERKEGAARD: Patience, Socrates. How un-Socratic of you to be the impatient party in the dialog!

SOCRATES: Hmph! Well, if this is the way in which your analogy is inaccurate, what is the way in which it is accurate?

KIERKEGAARD: By this new birth the man is indeed enabled to perform acts which human nature alone cannot perform.

SOCRATES: What acts?

KIERKEGAARD: Can't you guess?

SOCRATES: You are playing games with me.

KIERKEGAARD: I am. Two games: mine and yours. As you are playing one of them with me, yours.

SOCRATES: Let us play, then. I will guess that since the act you have in mind is an act that is natural only for a god, and is beyond the nature of a mere man, it is to be able to live forever, in Heaven, with the God.

KIERKEGAARD: A good guess, Socrates.

SOCRATES: So do you believe that immortality is not part of human nature, but needs to be attained by this "new birth," so that some men have it and some do not? So all my proofs of the natural immortality of the soul—there were three of them in the "Phaedo" and a better one in the "Republic"—have a false conclusion?

KIERKEGAARD: In one sense yes, in another sense no. I do not deny what you meant by the natural immortality of every human soul.

SOCRATES: So you agree with me that the soul is not made of matter . . .

KIERKEGAARD: Yes.

SOCRATES: —so that when the material body falls apart the soul does not fall apart.

KIERKEGAARD: I agree.

SOCRATES: Even if this is a soul that has not experienced the "new birth."

KIERKEGAARD: Yes.

SOCRATES: Then what does this "new birth" give to the soul? I thought it was immortality.

KIERKEGAARD: It gives to the soul exactly what you said, Socrates: the ability to live in Heaven with God, the ability to see God's face and live. This is not mere survival, it is bliss.

SOCRATES: So there is another kind of immortality then, one without Heavenly bliss?

KIERKEGAARD: Yes.

SOCRATES: A Hell as well as a Heaven.

KIERKEGAARD: Yes.

SOCRATES: I am skeptical of that, you know. But I suppose we need not explore that now. But regarding the soul's ability to live in Heaven, are you saying that the soul did not have that ability before the "new birth"?

KIERKEGAARD: That is correct.

SOCRATES: That I do not understand.

KIERKEGAARD: That is because you were a Greek.

SOCRATES: What else could I have been?

KIERKEGAARD: There once was a people who knew the true God, the God you always sought, and hoped for, but never claimed to know. This people believed that no man could see God's face and live without God performing a miracle.

SOCRATES: And that miracle is what you call the "new birth"?

KIERKEGAARD: Yes.

SOCRATES: So that is the greater immortality, while mere survival of death is the lesser.

KIERKEGAARD: Yes.

SOCRATES: So we all have by nature the lesser immortality but not the greater.

KIERKEGAARD: Yes.

SOCRATES: I see. Is there any other godlike act which you believe the soul can perform only after the "new birth?" Can it perform miracles, perhaps, like a god?

KIERKEGAARD: They sometimes happen. But they are not in the soul's own power, or at the behest of its own will, so when they do happen it is only because the God has empowered the soul through the new birth to become a possible *instrument* of His miraculous action.

But miracles are not universal, or even common. More importantly, they are not *important*. Not even the most spectacular of miracles is even infinitesimally important compared to the act which is the whole point of the "new birth," the whole end and purpose of it.

SOCRATES: And what is that?

KIERKEGAARD: It is one thing, though it has three names: Faith, Hope, and Love. These are really three aspects of a single thing: the openness on the part of the creature to the real presence of the God, who enters the soul as a knight might enter a city, by the gate called Faith, grasps and lifts up the humble maiden onto his horse by the arm of Hope, and spurs the three of them down the road and through the whole city with all-conquering speed in the journey called Love, or Charity.

SOCRATES: Are these feelings?

KIERKEGAARD: No, they are acts of the will.

SOCRATES: The human will?

KIERKEGAARD: Yes, though they are also gifts of the divine will, gifts of grace.

SOCRATES: I think you just contradicted yourself.

KIERKEGAARD: How?

SOCRATES: You said that this human act of will allows the God to enter the soul. So this human act must precede the divine one, unless the God enters the soul by force, against man's will.

SOCRATES MEETS KIERKEGAARD

KIERKEGAARD: No, He does not do that. He seduces but He does not rape.

SOCRATES: But you also said that unless the God enters the soul, the soul cannot perform this act. It is a gift of grace.

KIERKEGAARD: That is also true.

SOCRATES: How can the same human act be both prior to and posterior to the divine act? How can it be both a cause and an effect of the divine act? That sounds like an impossibility, a contradiction.

KIERKEGAARD: It would indeed be a contradiction if we were asking about the relationship between two events in time. But the act of the God is eternal, though its human effect is in time, because the God is eternal— not just beginningless and endless but timeless. So from His point of view, it is one thing, one event: the divine grace by which faith and hope and love are given as gifts to man, and the man's free choice to receive these gifts.

SOCRATES: I do not understand this, but I do not want to wander too far into metaphysical questions about how God sees this event when I am not sure I understand what it is even from the human side. Let me try again. When I asked whether this "new birth" produced an accidental change in the soul or an essential change, you said it was not an accidental change, but not an essential change of species either, but another kind of essential change, in which a second nature is added to man's first nature without replacing it. Is that correct?

KIERKEGAARD: Yes.

SOCRATES: So it is as if a man digested a pig without the pig being destroyed, so that the man would be both a pig and a man at the same time.

KIERKEGAARD: Something like that.

SOCRATES: So the human nature of the man who receives this second nature from the God is not destroyed but perfected.

KIERKEGAARD: Yes.

SOCRATES: So it is not a change of species in the soul. The soul is still the humble maiden, but it is now riding the horse of the Heavenly knight, to use your poetic analogy.

KIERKEGAARD: Yes—but even that analogy is not perfect because in the analogy the maiden is only *on* the horse and *in the arms of* the knight. It is an external change. But the new birth is an internal change in the soul, like pregnancy in the body, though its cause is external, as a husband is external to his wife.

SOCRATES: Might you say, then, to make your analogy more accurate, that the maiden and the horse become a single new creature, a centaur, half human and half horse?

KIERKEGAARD: That analogy too has both true and false aspects. It is true that the transformation is inward and that it adds something to the soul rather than destroying it. But a centaur is only half human, not wholly human, and only half horse, not wholly horse. It is a monster. The newly-born soul is wholly human, not half human, though it also has divine life.

SOCRATES: I cannot understand that. How can one be

both human and divine, both a man and a god, at the same time?

KIERKEGAARD: If you had ever met this Man, you would know that it is possible, even though you would not know how.

SOCRATES: That is not a satisfying answer to me. Nor is your original analogy. What is this "new birth"? Is it only a figure of speech, an exaggeration?

KIERKEGAARD: No.

SOCRATES: Is it literal, then? Surely a man cannot enter into his mother's womb a second time.

KIERKEGAARD: That is exactly what another philosopher once said when first told of the new birth.

SOCRATES: Did this philosopher also express consternation, as I did? Did he say, "How can such things be?"

KIERKEGAARD: That is exactly what he said.

SOCRATES: Then does this "new birth" mean Reincarnation—the same soul getting a new body after death? I toyed with that idea, as did many of my fellow Greeks, and called it a "likely story," though I did not claim to *know* that it was true.

KIERKEGAARD: No, that is not what it means at all. That is what a Hindu or a Buddhist would say, separating body and soul into two substances.

SOCRATES: That is also what I did, for if body and soul are two substances, this explains the soul's immortality. For if body and soul are like oil and water, then the fire that destroys the oil does not destroy the water, and the evaporation that destroys the water does not

}78{

destroy the oil. But you said that that is *not* what you mean.

KIERKEGAARD: No. The teaching I speak of came not from Greece or India or China but from Israel.

SOCRATES: Your "Teacher," then, was a Jew.

KIERKEGAARD: Yes. And the Jews were just about the only people in the world who did not believe in Reincarnation.

SOCRATES: A strange people, with strange stories.

But I still do not understand this "new birth." Are there other ways of describing it?

KIERKEGAARD: Yes. Let us look at some other names for it. One of them is "conversion."

In so far as he was in Error, he was constantly in the act of departing from the Truth . . . in consequence of receiving the condition in the Moment, the course of his life has been given an opposite direction, so that he is turned about. Let us call this change *Conversion*, even though this word has not been hitherto used; but that is precisely a reason for choosing it, in order thereby to avoid confusion, for it is as if expressly coined for the change we have in mind.

SOCRATES: Surely you are being ironic here, for you must know that a conversion, a fundamental turn of one's whole life, is precisely the thing I myself sought to provoke in my dialogs, especially long ones like the "Gorgias." And when Plato wrote about this "turning" in the "Republic," in that famous parable of the Cave, "conversion" was precisely the word he used for it. So the word *has* been used, both in religion and in philosophy.

KIERKEGAARD: As you say, I am being ironic here.

SOCRATES: But what is the point of this irony? Is it that I am closer to you than I think because I too saw the need for a total "conversion," a 180-degree turn? Or is it the opposite point: that although the term is common to the two of us, the two realities designated by this term are much farther apart than I can possibly understand?

KIERKEGAARD: Might it not be both?

SOCRATES: You are as tricky as I was! You work (or play) with the mind of your student on many different levels at the same time. Are you yourself the Teacher you speak of?

KIERKEGAARD: Hush! What a stupid thought that is! Your first really stupid thought, Socrates. And I am not now being ironic or tricky. That was a blasphemous thought, for I already said that the Teacher is the God.

SOCRATES: I thought perhaps you were suggesting that the soul itself was a god.

KIERKEGAARD: *You* might have suggested that, Socrates—I'm not sure—but certainly not I.

SOCRATES: Thank you for being very clear. No divine souls, then, and no Reincarnation. Please go on, then.

KIERKEGAARD: In so far as the learner was in Error by reason of his own guilt, this conversion cannot take place without being taken up in his consciousness, or without his becoming aware that his former state was a consequence of his guilt. With this consciousness he will then take leave of his former state. But what leave-taking is without a sense of sadness? The sadness in this case, however, is on account of his having so long remained in his former state. Let us call such grief *Repentance;* for what is Repentance but a kind of leave-taking, a looking backward indeed, but in such a way as precisely to quicken the steps to that which lies before?

SOCRATES: That is clear, I think. But the "new birth" still is not.

KIERKEGAARD: **In so far as the learner was in Error, and now receives the Truth and with it the condition for understanding it, a change takes place within him like the change from non-being to being . . .**

SOCRATES: But it doesn't! Learning the truth is not like being born. What an absurd image! Unless . . .

KIERKEGAARD: Yes? I think you are beginning to discover my trick, however carefully I hid it under misleadingly Greek words.

SOCRATES: Unless you mean by Truth something other than the *definitions* I sought, the *Forms* Plato posited.

KIERKEGAARD: You're getting closer. What might that be, do you think?

SOCRATES: Perhaps it is something more like your own "true" being, as a caterpillar attains its true being only when it becomes a butterfly. True *being* rather than just true *thought.*

KIERKEGAARD: You have discovered my secret, or half of it, anyway. The Hebrew word for Truth—"emeth"—suggests just that, for it is predicated not of ideas but of persons, first of all of God. It means "totally trustable, reliable, full of integrity, always keeping his promises." Your Greek word for Truth—"aletheia"—means "not forgetting" and suggests something much more intellectual. In fact it suggests your whole philosophy of Recollection, "Anamnesis," which is part of your hypothesis "A."

SOCRATES: Yes, for "aletheia" contains "Lethe," the river of forgetfulness which each soul must drink when it leaves the body at death, according to our sacred story.

KIERKEGAARD: But *our* sacred stories are very different than yours. They point not to a merely mental change—remembering the timeless truths which had been forgotten—or even merely a moral change—obeying better moral laws, or obeying them a bit better—but an ontological change, a change in being, in reality, in existence—in fact, the most radical change in one's life: being born, coming into existence. Thus I say:

A change takes place in him like the change from non-being to being. But this transition from non-being to being is the transition we call birth. Now one who exists (already) cannot be born (into existence); nevertheless the disciple is born. Let us call this transition the *New Birth*, in consequence of which the disciple enters the world quite as at the first birth, an individual human being knowing nothing as yet about the world into which he is born.

SOCRATES: I see the great gap between my sacred story and yours. For me it is all about forgetting and remembering.

KIERKEGAARD: But there is also a similarity there. I say: **Just as one who has begotten himself by the aid of the Socratic midwifery now forgets everything else in** the world, and . . . forgets the world in his discovery of himself, so the latter (the one who has been born again) forgets himself in the discovery of his Teacher.

SOCRATES: So both conversions are forgettings, and leave-takings, for in both a whole world is left behind.

KIERKEGAARD: Yes.

SOCRATES: But what is found in each case is very different. In my case it is not the teacher but the self. It is the fulfillment of the quest to "know thyself." But in your case it is precisely the Teacher that is found.

KIERKEGAARD: Yes. But also the self.

SOCRATES: How can that be?

KIERKEGAARD: It is found only by losing it, by giving it away to the Teacher.

SOCRATES: I do not know what that means.

KIERKEGAARD: Even so, you see that there is self-forgetting in my story as well as yours.

SOCRATES: I think there is also a finding of the self in my story, and not just a finding of true definitions of the Forms. My dialectic also aimed at what you called "emeth," a higher kind of "truth." It was not just a truer *thought* but a truer *person* that I aimed for.

KIERKEGAARD: Yes. You see now how I was deliberately equivocating in using the word "truth." It was my puzzle, and you solved it, just as you solved the puzzle the Delphic oracle gave you. You are an excellent puzzle solver, Socrates.

SOCRATES: It took me a lifetime to solve *that* puzzle.

For it seemed a simple self-contradiction for the oracle to tell a man who knew he had no wisdom at all that no one on earth was wiser than he.

KIERKEGAARD: See? What *you think* is a self-contradiction may not be.

SOCRATES: Yes—since what I think is not identical with truth.

KIERKEGAARD: That is a simple but rare lesson, and most of us find it bitter and hard to learn. And that is one of the simplest proofs that we are in Error, as my story says. But you learned this lesson so well that it was always Lesson One for you.

SOCRATES: So this may also be true about your strange story as well as the oracle's—this story that you call the "thought-experiment" of "B," and which is nothing more nor less than what the world calls the Christian religion, if I am not mistaken.

KIERKEGAARD: You are not mistaken about the label, at least.

SOCRATES: Let's see if I am mistaken about Truth. I will try to sort out the different meanings of that word in your story, your riddle. (By the way, that is how you categorize your religion, is it not?—as a story or a riddle rather than a philosophy?)

KIERKEGAARD: Yes. It is perceptive of you to see that fact, Socrates.

SOCRATES: I only wish I could comprehend the content as well as the category. Well, perhaps it would help if I distinguished the different meanings of "truth" as you use the word in your telling of the story, or the riddle, *as if* it were a philosophy alternative to mine.

I think I need to distinguish *four* kinds of truth in order to understand you. All four have been part of our conversation here from the beginning, present in a confused way, even though we thought—I thought, anyway—that it was only one kind of Truth we were discussing.

There is first of all **temporal, empirical truth,** "facts." And this kind of truth we were *not* discussing, but rising above—unless this "new birth" of yours is included in this category. Perhaps it is. Perhaps your irony is that this apparently lowest kind of truth, the truth of changing events in time, is the highest! You do speak of the radical newness of the "new birth," after all, and the importance of "the Moment."

Perhaps I was wrong about the content of this category. I characterized this kind of truth, the truth that changes with time, merely as empirical truth, the truth of things we can perceive with our senses—visible changes—but that was a mistake, I think, since the human spirit, or mind, or soul, also changes, and this "new birth" of yours is just such a change. It is an event, but it is not visible, not empirical.

Second, there are Platonic Forms, timeless truths, which I tried to define in words, in formulas or definitions. Each of my dialogs is such a hunting expedition. Such definitions we could call **epistemological truth.**

Third, there is one's true self, or authentic self. We might call this **psychological or anthropological truth.** Only now, after we have read your whole chapter, do we understand that this kind of truth was what you meant from the beginning, when you asked "How far does the Truth admit of being learned?" Since you contrasted your answer with mine, you seemed to be hunting the same quarry as I was—what I called "epistemological truth"—but in fact that expedition was only a spy's disguise for what you were really hunting: the truth of one's true self, which you say comes only by this "new birth."

But now, at the very moment when we seem to understood each other, and met at the summit of our climb, we must part again in misunderstanding. For you now point to *another* summit, I think, and there is a deep gap between the two summits. For this fourth kind of Truth seems to be the Teacher himself, who is the God, rather than the true self of the human soul. We might call this fourth kind of truth "**theological truth**," but I think that is misleading, for if I understand you correctly you do not mean truth *about* God that exists *in* a human mind, but a truth that exists in the divine Teacher Himself. And this must mean something more than merely the third kind of truth, personal authenticity; for that kind of truth can exist in a man as well as in a god; while this fourth kind of truth can exists only in the God. Is that not so?

KIERKEGAARD: You understand me very well. All human teachers said that they taught the truth, but this divine Teacher of mine said, "I AM the Truth."

SOCRATES: Alas, then I do not understand you at all. For how a *person,* even a divine person, can *be* the Truth, I must confess I have not the foggiest idea. Surely it is a category confusion if a person, human or divine, says "I AM the Truth?"

KIERKEGAARD: "Surely"? What has become of your famous Socratic questioning of every assumption?

SOCRATES: I am abashed and ashamed to be hoist by my own petard again. But *whatever* this fourth kind of truth might mean, is this the point you want to finally bring us?

KIERKEGAARD: It is. And it is not a "point" but a Person.

SOCRATES: Perhaps I can begin to understand you if I return to your text.

KIERKEGAARD: That is why we are here, I think.

7.
Kierkegaard's Argument for Believing the Christian Alternative to Socrates

SOCRATES: Can you give me any reason for believing this strange story of yours, this fantastic "thought-experiment"?

KIERKEGAARD: That is what I do in the last three long paragraphs of my first chapter.

SOCRATES: Finally! Reasons are something I *can* understand. I am beginning to feel a little more comfortable.

KIERKEGAARD: Ah, but I think you will find it to be a very strange *kind* of reason, as the thought-experiment is a strange *kind* of thought-experiment.

SOCRATES: That feeling of comfort lasted somewhat less than a minute!

KIERKEGAARD: I begin by asking the expected question: **But is the hypothesis here expounded thinkable?**

SOCRATES: And by "thinkable" do you mean "understandable" or "believable"?

KIERKEGAARD: Both—for one cannot believe a thing unless he has at least a partial understanding of it.

SOCRATES: But then you give an unexpected answer, an unexpected *sort* of answer. Instead of "yes" or "no" or "perhaps," you answer this question with another question.

KIERKEGAARD: Yes, for my Teacher was a rabbi.

SOCRATES: What is a rabbi?

KIERKEGAARD: One who asks questions like this one: "Why does a rabbi always answer a question with another question?"

SOCRATES: It is because the poor rabbi has met me and caught my good infection?

KIERKEGAARD: The answer is: "Why *shouldn't* a rabbi answer a question with another question?" That is the only answer that is consistent with the question, you see. Similarly, in all your dialogs you too answer your initial question with other questions.

SOCRATES: Thus I reverse the roles of the teacher and the learner. The one who asks questions—myself—is really the teacher. And I am a teacher of others only by being first a student, a student of truth, and a student of truth is one who asks questions of truth, his teacher.

KIERKEGAARD: Yes, but it is more than that. A rabbi does indeed teach by questioning, as you do, and he thus turns around the roles of teacher and student, as you do. But *my* rabbi also turns around the question itself from something impersonal to something personal, so that the student finds himself not merely the one who is asking the question but the one who is being asked.

SOCRATES: What does that mean?

KIERKEGAARD: I shall show you by an example. It is in the next thing I wrote. I answer the question I asked, the question of whether the hypothesis is thinkable, by asking another question, but this other question is a question about the *who*, not just about the *what*:

Let us not be in haste to reply. . . . Before we reply, let us ask ourselves from whom we may expect an answer to our question.

This is a crucial turn, I think, it is not the words themselves that I question, nor the logical presupposition behind them, but the person who utters them, the person who answers my question—or, more precisely, the right of this person to give an answer.

Thus my dialog partner is no longer an impersonal, universal spectator, an "everyone and no one," detached from the truth he utters; but he is sucked into the situation like the apparently-safe, shore-bound observer of hurricane waves being suddenly swept out to sea by them. It is no longer a question that allows personal detachment; it is now one that demands personal involvement.

SOCRATES: I think I understand your deliciously dastardly plot and your delightfully deceitful ploy.

KIERKEGAARD: That is because it takes a thief to catch a thief.

SOCRATES: So how do you then answer your question whether your hypothesis is thinkable, which has now turned into the question *"For whom* is it thinkable?"

KIERKEGAARD: By an analogy:

The being born, is this fact thinkable? Certainly, why not? But for whom is it thinkable, for one who is born, or for one who is not born? The latter supposition is an absurdity which could never have entered anyone's head. . . . When one has experienced birth thinks of himself as born, he conceives this transition from non-being to being . . .

SOCRATES: So this "new birth" is like physical birth in that it is something we can understand only by experience, a posteriori, not something we can understand a priori, as a timeless possibility, a kind of Platonic Idea?

KIERKEGAARD: Exactly. No angel, no spirit, no god who was conceived simply by the thought of another god, could imagine or invent this thing we all take for granted, human birth. So I then reason, by analogy, that The same principle must also hold in the case of the new birth . . . who then may be expected to think the new birth? Surely the man who has himself been born anew, since it would of course be absurd to imagine that one not so born could think it. Would it not be the height of the ridiculous for such an individual to entertain this notion?

SOCRATES: So you are arguing that since the notion of the new birth exists in the minds of at least some men, as a subjective event, it must exist in reality, as an objective event, since everything requires an adequate cause, and the adequate cause for this idea, this mental event, could only be the actual experience of it, as a fact, rather than the mere mental invention of it, as a fantasy.

KIERKEGAARD: Yes. Do you have any objections to this reasoning?

SOCRATES: I think that you will have to answer some hard questions from thinkers who will arise after you, especially one named Freud, if you are to defend this argument. Perhaps there are ways in which the idea *could* arise as a dream, or a fantasy. But that conversation must be put off until another day.

KIERKEGAARD: There is no shortage of days here, is there?

SOCRATES: No.

KIERKEGAARD: I know nothing about this man Freud, but I know and respect you and your use of logic, Socrates. Do *you* have any objection to my reasoning?

SOCRATES: I certainly have no objection to your *principle*, your assumption that every event, mental as well as physical, must have a sufficient cause. But I wonder what was in fact the cause of this thought—the thought of the "new birth," the thought of what you call hypothesis "B." Are you arguing that since you think the thought, you must have experienced the fact? Must the idea have originated with you? Could it not be copied from someone else, plagiarized, so to speak?

KIERKEGAARD: Indeed it could. Your suspicion is quite correct: the idea did not originate with me. But, then, where *did* it originate? That is precisely my next question, the question of the next paragraph. And that is my argument for its truth: Your very objection against it (that it is a case of plagiarism) is an argument *for* it:

There you have my project. But I think I hear someone say: "This is the most ridiculous of all projects; or rather, you are of all projectors of hypotheses the most ridiculous. For even when a man propounds something nonsensical (which is how you confess my hypothesis appears to you), it may still remain true that it is he who has propounded it; but you behave like a lazzarone who takes money for exhibiting premises open to everybody's inspection; you are like the man who collected a fee for exhibiting a ram in the afternoon, which in the forenoon could be seen gratis, grazing in the open field."

Perhaps it is so; I hide my head in shame. But assuming that I am as ridiculous as you say, let me try to make amends by proposing a new hypothesis. Everybody knows that gunpowder was invented centuries ago, and in so far it would be ridiculous of me to pretend to be the inventor; but would it be equally ridiculous of me to assume that somebody was the inventor? Now I am going to be so polite as to assume that you are the author of my project; greater politeness than this you can scarcely ask. Or if you deny this, will you also deny that someone is the author, that is to say, some human being? In that case I am as near to being the author as any other human being. So that your anger is not vented upon me because I appropriated something that belongs to another human being, but because I appropriated something of which no human being is the rightful owner; and hence your anger is by no means appeased when I deceitfully ascribe that authorship to you.

Is it not strange that there should be something such in existence to which everyone who knows it knows also that he has not invented it; and that this "pass-me-by" neither stops nor can be stopped even if we ask all men in turn? This strange fact deeply impresses me, and casts over me a spell; for it constitutes a test of the hypothesis and proves its truth.

SOCRATES: You are exaggerating here, I think, when you say "proves," are you not?

KIERKEGAARD: No, for exaggeration is a quantitative "more" of something within a single genus. My point in saying the hypothesis is "proved" is not that it is very highly probable, for that is a mere quantitative exaggeration within the genus of logical probability. My argument has nothing to do with calculating probabilities. It is in another genus. It is more personal than the calculating of probabilities, for it is about the authority of personal experience; and it is more certain than calculating probabilities, since it rests on the certain principle of causality, as you correctly perceived: the principle that a mental as well as a physical event must have an adequate cause.

SOCRATES: Is your logic then inductive or deductive?

KIERKEGAARD: It is neither. It is seductive.

SOCRATES: Hmm. A new kind of logic! Go on, then, with your seduction..

KIERKEGAARD: **It would certainly be absurd to expect of a man that he should of his own accord discover that he did not exist.**

SOCRATES: That is true. That is the whole point of Descartes' "I think, therefore I am." It would be self-contradictory to say "I do not exist" because only an existing thing can think that it does not exist *or* that it does.

KIERKEGAARD: But this argument of Descartes' is not a logical self-contradiction but an existential one. The idea that Descartes does not exist is not self-contradictory at all. In fact it is true, at every moment after Descartes' death or before his conception. Only an existing "I" can think or say "I," and therefore he contradicts himself if he says he does not exist only because the logical content of his words is contradicted by the existential fact of his being there to say them.

SOCRATES: That is precisely what I tried to point out to him.

KIERKEGAARD: You cross-examined Descartes?

SOCRATES: Yes, not too long ago.

KIERKEGAARD: How I would have enjoyed hearing that conversation!

SOCRATES: You will be able to do so, in good time. This is the place where nothing good is lost. But first, what is the next step of your argument?

KIERKEGAARD: I next say: **But this** (a man's discovery that he did not exist before) **is precisely the transition of the new birth, from non-being to being.**

SOCRATES: But one must already exist before he can be reborn, is this not so?

KIERKEGAARD: Yes.

SOCRATES: And thus there is a difference between the two births, and the two modes of existence, the physical and the spiritual.

KIERKEGAARD: Yes. Though I would not say "the physical and the spiritual," for the first birth is already the birth of a being with a soul as well as a body.

SOCRATES: I accept your correction. But your analogy between the "new birth" and the old birth does not hold, then. They are different.

KIERKEGAARD: They are indeed different, but the analogy does hold, as I pointed out in the previous paragraph, where after noting the difference between the two births, I asked: **Or is the difficulty increased by the fact that the non-being which precedes the new birth contains more being than the non-being which preceded the first birth?** That was a rhetorical question.

SOCRATES: I see. The analogy holds because it is the same principle of causality which governs both events.

KIERKEGAARD: Exactly. Thus I conclude:

Be then angry with me and with whoever else pretends to the authorship of this thought; but that is no reason why you should be angry with the thought itself.

SOCRATES: This "thought," of course, is Christianity.

KIERKEGAARD: Precisely.

SOCRATES: But Christianity is not a "hypothesis."

KIERKEGAARD: Indeed. It is an historical event.

SOCRATES: Is it the event that happened two millennia ago in Bethlehem, the event you call the "Incarnation" of the God, or the event that happens today whenever any man experiences this "new birth"?

KIERKEGAARD: It is the same event.

SOCRATES: You mean the event of the eternal divine nature entering time and joining with a human nature?

KIERKEGAARD: Yes.

SOCRATES: This event continues?

KIERKEGAARD: Yes. This gift of divine life comes to many people in history, again and again in time.

SOCRATES: But it must come from eternity, because it can come only from the God.

KIERKEGAARD: Yes, because of the same principle, the principle of causality: that nothing can give what it does not have.

SOCRATES: And therefore the only possible giver of the gift of a divine nature, or a divine life, must be the God Himself.

KIERKEGAARD: Yes.

SOCRATES: And this is your "Teacher," who is more than a teacher.

KIERKEGAARD: Yes. As you so incomparably perceived, a merely human teacher is like a midwife to the mind, an intellectual obstetrician, who merely helps his student bring to birth a truth from within, by the power of the student's own mind. Of this relationship between teacher and student I said that "between man and man this is the highest relationship." And because you perceived this so clearly and practiced it so consistently, I deem you the best of human teachers. But the Teacher of the New Birth is more than teacher. He is not merely the midwife for the soul; he is her husband, who impregnates her with his life.

SOCRATES: Your hypothesis "B" is all very consistent internally. But that does not mean it is true. A fairy tale may also be consistent—in fact, if it is not, it is a poorly told tale—but that does not mean it is true.

KIERKEGAARD: Then let us look at this Christian thing—which I looked at under the misleading but instructive category of a hypothesis, or a thought-experiment, or a philosophy, in my first chapter—let us look at it under the equally misleading but equally instructive category of a fairy tale. That is what I do in the next chapter.

SOCRATES: So you use even a falsehood or a fallacy—that Christianity is a philosophy, or that it is a myth, a fairy tale—to teach the truth.

KIERKEGAARD: That is precisely my strategy.

SOCRATES: You are as tricky as the oracle of a god!

8.
The Gospel as Fairy Tale

SOCRATES: In your first chapter, which you called "A Project of Thought," you transposed your religion into the form of a philosophy in order to compare and contrast it with mine. You turned your faith-experiment into a thought-experiment, as if your divine Teacher was having a philosophical conversation with me in the Agora about Truth and how we learn it. This "as if" is the reason you call it a thought-experiment, or "a project of thought," or a hypothesis, isn't that so?

KIERKEGAARD: It is so.

SOCRATES: Let me see whether I have understood the difference between your hypothesis and mine in terms of my distinction between four kinds of truth. If your Teacher is right, we do not just *learn*, by thought, the truth, either in the first, empirical sense of "truth" or in the second, Platonic sense, but we *become* it, in the "new birth." And this is "truth" in the third, anthropological sense.

KIERKEGAARD: So far, so good.

SOCRATES: And because of the principle of causality, because you cannot give what you do not have, your Teacher must somehow *be* the truth by His own eternal nature—and that is the fourth sense of "truth." When He gives this gift of Himself somehow to us, in time, this fourth kind of truth becomes the third kind of truth, or what I have called anthropological truth, our true being as humans who somehow share in the divine nature or divine life—whatever that may mean. Do I understand you correctly here?

KIERKEGAARD: Yes.

SOCRATES: This is an astonishing thought, that staggers the reason.

KIERKEGAARD: It also staggers the imagination. That is why in my next chapter I present it as what I call "An Essay of the *Imagination*" rather than "A Project of *Thought*."

SOCRATES: So you transpose your Christian religion into a second pagan Greek form, namely a myth, a sacred story, which is a kind of parable or allegory or true fiction.

KIERKEGAARD: That is my strategy, yes.

SOCRATES: And you imply that this sacred story of the imagination, like the "thought experiment" of your first chapter, comes not from man but from God, when you contrast its teaching with mine again, at the beginning of this chapter. And you do this by contrasting the *equality* between the Socratic teacher and his student (both being human) with the *inequality* between the divine Teacher and His human student or disciple. You say:

As between man and man no higher relationship is possible (than the Socratic relationship): the disciple gives occasion for the teacher to understand himself *and* the teacher gives occasion for the disciple to understand himself. (I think both of these processes have been going on here between us!) **When the teacher dies he leaves behind him no claim upon the soul of the disciple** (since the disciple merely recollected the truth that was already in him from the beginning). . . . **But the God needs no disciple to help him understand himself.** So that relationship is not reciprocal.

You then ask the crucial question: **What then could move him to make his appearance? He must indeed move himself, and continue to exemplify what Aristotle says of him: "the unmoved mover of all things." But if he moves himself it follows that he is not moved by some need, as if he could not endure the strain of silence but had to break out in speech. But if he moves himself, and is not moved by need, what else can move him but love?**

But I ask you, is not love the greatest of needs?

KIERKEGAARD: That is true of *eros*, the kind of love you spoke of so eloquently, especially in the "Symposium," as well as for all other kinds of love except one. And that one is the one I speak of here. It is called "*agape*."

SOCRATES: In my language and in my day, that word had little meaning. It was usually used as a generic term for any kind of love at all; and therefore we Greeks, who preferred clear and specific terms rather than vague generic ones, used it very little, especially when we wanted to be clear and to distinguish one thing from another. Are you being deliberately vague here?

KIERKEGAARD: Exactly the opposite. For my Teacher said that the whole world would recognize His disciples, and the radical difference between them and all other men—the difference between the twice-born and the once-born—by the fact that His disciples would have this *agape*.

SOCRATES: How can the generic be that which differentiates? That is logically impossible.

KIERKEGAARD: It is indeed. His disciples put a radically new meaning into that old, fuzzy, almost useless word *agape* to describe His radically new kind of love. It was not the old generic meaning but a newly specific meaning that distinguished this *agape* from other kinds of love.

SOCRATES: And what is that distinction?

KIERKEGAARD: It is gift-love, not need-love.

SOCRATES: But surely other human loves can be gift-loves too, as well as need-loves? For instance the love of a human mother for her baby is both gift-love and need-love, for mothers need children, both physically and emotionally, as well as being needed by them, though in a different way. The same is obviously true of men and women: their loves for each other are both selfish and unselfish.

KIERKEGAARD: This is true. In fact, that is why *agape* is distinctive: it is pure gift love.

SOCRATES: I see. I wonder if that is possible.

KIERKEGAARD: Not from human nature alone, no. You are right about human nature: in it all loves are at least partly need-loves.

SOCRATES: Does the difference between *agape* and need-love match the difference between body and soul?

KIERKEGAARD: No. The difference applies to both bodily loves and soulish loves. Bodies can be given as pure gifts, by martyrdom. And there is need in the soulish loves that come from human nature alone, from the once-born. For souls need truth as much as bodies need food.

SOCRATES: How is it possible that there can be in us a pure gift-love without needs? We are never without needs.

KIERKEGAARD: It is possible because it comes from a perfect God, who has by nature no needs. Indeed no man is free of needs, so if *agape* exists, it could only come from God.

SOCRATES: And so if it did exist, it would be the strongest and most concrete proof of the reality of such a God, a God of pure unselfish love.

KIERKEGAARD: That is why the Christian proof of the existence of God is the existence of Christ, the God in time.

SOCRATES: But to say that it *could* come only from the God is not to say that it *does*.

KIERKEGAARD: True. But if the God is so powerful that He can produce anything—anything that is meaningful, anything that is not simply logically self-contradictory, like a green frog that is not green or not a frog—then He *could* produce this pure gift-love and bestow it upon unworthy recipients such as us.

SOCRATES: But why would He do this? He could also produce a hundred-mile-long island comprised entirely of grains of orange rice. But there is no reason for Him to do this. And if He is the perfect God, He cannot be unreasonable.

KIERKEGAARD: What do you mean by saying that He cannot be unreasonable? Surely He could *seem* to us to be unreasonable, if He knows so much more than we do—as a parent seems unreasonable to a child, though it is really the child that is unreasonable.

SOCRATES: You are right. I did not mean *that*. In fact, if the God did *not* ever seem at all unreasonable to us, then his mind would be no different than our mind, and he would not be a god after all. But even the God cannot produce something that is self-contradictory and thus meaningless. Do you say that He could produce a frog that is not a frog?

KIERKEGAARD: I don't want to say that, but I don't want to deny it either. It seems a bit presumptuous.

SOCRATES: I think it is much *more* presumptuous for us to say that "God is omnipotent, therefore He can do anything, therefore he can produce a frog that is not a frog."

KIERKEGAARD: Why?

SOCRATES: Because that is a kind of mere word magic, claiming that you have changed a literally meaningless phrase into one that is meaningful just by the addition of the words "God can" from outside.

KIERKEGAARD: I'm not sure about that.

SOCRATES: Then do you claim that a set of meaningless words suddenly becomes meaningful when you add to them the other words "God can do this"?

KIERKEGAARD: No.

SOCRATES: Then God could not be unreasonable.

KIERKEGAARD: In the sense that He could not be something that is simply and really self-contradictory, and therefore simply and really and literally meaningless, yes.

SOCRATES: Do you also agree that He could not *act* unreasonably?

KIERKEGAARD: I agree that He could not both produce a hundred-mile-long island of orange rice and not produce it at the same time. But I do not agree that He could not produce it.

SOCRATES: Would He have sufficient reason for producing it, if He did produce it?

KIERKEGAARD: He would. But that reason may not be known to us, or appear reasonable to us. This is what I call "the acoustical illusion," in which we unconsciously project our own limitations onto the God, so that we seem to be hearing from Him something irrational, merely because it is something that in us would be irrational. We think we hear the irrationality of the God while we are in fact hearing our own.

SOCRATES: And you think that this pure gift-love, this *agape,* is such a thing?

KIERKEGAARD: Yes. That is not impossible, is it?

SOCRATES: You mean that my skepticism of *agape* is an acoustical illusion?

KIERKEGAARD: Yes, that is what I mean.

SOCRATES: Yes, I admit it is possible.

KIERKEGAARD: Then we can perform this second thought-experiment, even though we do not know yet whether it is true or false, since it is at least *possible*. I can tell the story of the God's *agape* for man, which is the Gospel, the "good news," which constitutes the very essence of my religion.

SOCRATES: All right. But here is another thing I cannot comprehend. The God must be eternal and changeless, if He is perfect. For if He changes, He must become either better or worse, both of which are impossible for absolute perfection. But you say the God is in time, producing this "new birth" in "the Moment." Which is it? Is the God in time or outside of time?

KIERKEGAARD: Both! His will is eternal, and is not caused by temporal events, as temporal events are caused by each other. But the realization of His eternal will *for* time takes place *in* time. He acts *on* time and even *in* time but *from* eternity. As I say, **His resolve, which stands in no equal reciprocal relation to the occasion, must be from eternity, though when realized in time it constitutes precisely the *Moment*.**

SOCRATES: I think I just barely understand that. Go on with your story, then.

KIERKEGAARD: **Moved by love, the God is thus eternally resolved to reveal himself. But as love is the motive so love must also be the end, for it would be a contradiction for the God to have a motive and an end which did not correspond.**

SOCRATES: That must be so, if he is eternal. But the

object of his love is man in time, rather than merely Himself in eternity—is that not part of your story?

KIERKEGAARD: It is. As I say, **His love is a love of the learner, and his aim is to win him.**

SOCRATES: What does this mean: "to win him"?

KIERKEGAARD: The aim of all love is always some kind of presence, some kind of union with the beloved, is it not?

SOCRATES: That is so. But how can there be union between two such unequal persons, the eternal, perfect God and the temporal, imperfect man?

KIERKEGAARD: That is precisely God's problem. Love seeks some kind of union, and therefore some kind of equality. And God and man are unequal, therefore they must be made equal somehow. And love not only seeks this, but love alone can attain it. **For it is only in love that the unequal can be made equal, and it is only in equality or unity that an understanding can be effected.**

SOCRATES: I do not see how love makes the unequal equal.

KIERKEGAARD: Naturally not, for you are only a man, and not the God. God once told a mystic that He had tried to teach man in just two very short propositions: (1) "I'm God." (2) "You're not."

SOCRATES: It is indeed strange that we find it so difficult to remember that second point! I will concede, then, that it is not impossible for the God to accomplish this somehow, though I cannot for the life of me see how.

I presume you believe also that since your God can accomplish this, he cannot experience unhappiness, as we mortals can, and as the gods of my culture could, since we made them in our own image. For unhappiness results from frustrated love, when what we love is absent or what we do not love is present.

KIERKEGAARD: No, I think I will surprise you again when I tell you that this God can indeed experience a kind of unhappiness in His love, once He leaves his eternal Heaven and steps into time. For while in eternity everything is actual, in time there is potentiality, and therefore passivity, and therefore the possibility of suffering. And that is what happens, in fact: the God suffers until His love is consummated.

SOCRATES: I find that indeed astonishing. In fact I cannot see how it is believable. It is like the paradox of your earlier "thought-experiment," the eternal Being, which is beginningless, getting a beginning in time. It looks like an intrinsic impossibility, a self-contradiction.

KIERKEGAARD: Again I must remind you of your own Lesson One, your famous humility, and of my mystic's Lesson Two: that you are not God.

SOCRATES: I accept both reminders But I still cannot comprehend your paradox, and why it is not a self-contradiction.

KIERKEGAARD: Patience, Socrates. Where is your famous patience?

SOCRATES: I never claimed to have patience. In fact, I often confessed the fault of impatience. For instance at the end of Book I of the "Republic" . . .

KIERKEGAARD: Excuse me for interrupting, but I think you said that before. Besides, we are here to explore my book rather than yours.

SOCRATES: Another needed reminder! What a fool I am—both forgetful and impatient. Back to your text, then. What is the next thing you say?

KIERKEGAARD: It is exactly the point I was making to you now, Socrates. I write: **Let us not jump too quickly to a conclusion at this point.**

SOCRATES: How uncanny—it is as if you were writing the book *to me* at every point, as if you had me before your eyes throughout the writing.

KIERKEGAARD: I did! And that is why I said earlier that perhaps this conversation is a test, or trial, or purgation, or learning experience, for both of us, rather than for one alone, as your dialogs were a trial only for the other party.

SOCRATES: Oh, they were that for me too, I'm sure.

KIERKEGAARD: Were you not a touchstone for everyone you met?

SOCRATES: Even if I was a touchstone, I was not like a stone, untouched, but like a friend, who is always touched and moved by his friend, for otherwise there is not friendship. But please go on with your thought-experiment.

KIERKEGAARD: **Much is heard in the world about unhappy love, and we all know what this means: the lovers are prevented from realizing their union, the causes being many and various. There is another kind of unhappy love, the theme of our present discourse, for which there is no perfect earthly parallel, though by dint** of speaking foolishly a little while we may make shift to conceive it through an earthly figure. The unhappiness of this love does not come from the inability of the lovers to realize their union but from their inability to understand each other. This grief is infinitely more profound than that of which men commonly speak, since it strikes at the very heart of love and wounds for an eternity; not like the other misfortune which touches only the temporal and the external. . . . This infinitely deeper grief is essentially the prerogative of the superior, since only he likewise understands the misunderstanding; in reality it belongs to the God alone, and no human relationship can afford a valid analogy. Nevertheless, we shall here suggest such an analogy, in order to quicken the mind to an apprehension of the divine.

SOCRATES: You speak of this unhappiness as a *prerogative*—"the prerogative of the superior." What a strange way to describe it. Why do you call suffering a "prerogative"?

KIERKEGAARD: Because I will no limit God. "With God all things are possible." Why should he be limited to happiness and be unable to experience unhappiness? Unhappiness in God is not a self-contradiction, like a frog that is not a frog.

SOCRATES: I cannot conceive what this would mean: for a perfect God to experience unhappiness. Can you explain this?

KIERKEGAARD: All we humans can do in attempting to answer that question about God—and perhaps *all* questions about God—is to use the best analogies, which are always human analogies rather than anything sub-human. For the human is closer to the super-human than the sub-human is.

Among men, then, which is the greater man: the one who is not capable of unhappiness, or the one who is?

SOCRATES: The one who is.

KIERKEGAARD: My case rests.

SOCRATES: Go on with your story, then.

KIERKEGAARD: Suppose there was a king who loved a humble maiden. But the reader has perhaps already lost his patience, seeing that our beginning sounds like a fairy tale, and is not in the least systematic. So the very learned Polus found it tiresome that Socrates always talked about meat and drink and doctors, and similar unworthy trifles, which Polus deemed beneath him. (*Gorgias*) But did not the Socratic manner of speech have at least one advantage, in that he himself and all others were from childhood equipped with the necessary prerequisites for understanding it? And would it not be desirable if I could confine the terms of my argument to meat and drink, and did not need to bring in kings, whose thoughts are not always like those of other men, if they are indeed kingly. But perhaps I may be pardoned this extravagance, seeing that I am only a poet.

SOCRATES: Your irony is not lost on me. Once again, you seem to have written every part of this book with me in mind. So our conversation is not an accident, but a fate. Go on.

KIERKEGAARD: Suppose then a king who loved a humble maiden. . . . It was easy to realize his purpose. Every statesman feared his wrath and dared not breathe a word of displeasure; every foreign state trembled before his power and dared not omit sending congratulations for the nuptials. . . . Then there awoke in the heart of the king an anxious thought; who but a king who thinks kingly thoughts would have dreamed of it! He spoke to no one about his anxiety; for if he had, each courtier would doubtless have said: "Your majesty is about to confer a favor upon the maiden, for which she can never be sufficiently grateful her whole life long." This speech would have moved the king to wrath, so that he would have commanded the execution of the courtier for high treason against the beloved, and thus he would in still another way have found his grief increased. So he wrestled with his troubled thoughts alone. Would she be happy in the life at his side? Would she be able to summon confidence enough never to remember what the king wished only to forget, that he was king and she had been a humble maiden? For if this memory were to waken in her soul, and like a favored lover sometimes steal her thoughts away from the king, luring her reflections into the seclusion of a secret grief; or if this memory sometimes passed through her soul like the shadow of death over the grave; where would then be the glory of their love? Then she would have been happier had she remained in her obscurity, loved by an equal, content in her humble cottage, but content in her love, cheerful early and late. What a rich abundance of grief is here laid bare! . . . And supposing she could not understand him? For while we are thus speaking foolishly of human relationships, we may suppose a difference of mind between them such as to render an understanding impossible . . .

You have not interrupted me for a long time, Socrates.

SOCRATES: Something in me is riveted by your strange story.

KIERKEGAARD: But if the Moment is to have decisive significance (and if not, we return to Socrates even if we think to advance beyond him), the learner is in Error, and that by reason of his own guilt. And yet he is the object of the God's love, and the God desires to teach him, and is concerned to bring him to equality with himself. If this equality cannot be established, the God's love becomes unhappy and his teaching meaningless, since they cannot understand each other.

SOCRATES: I fear that *we* do not understand each other. How can the God be unhappy if a God is perfect and unhappiness is an imperfection?

KIERKEGAARD: It could happen if perhaps unhappiness is *not* always an imperfection, as we supposed before. Suppose that the supreme perfection is not happiness but love, and the supreme imperfection not the lack of happiness but the lack of love. Suppose the word of love is not "happiness" but union; that the word of love is "better unhappy with her than happy without her"?

SOCRATES: A formidable set of suppositions!

KIERKEGAARD: But a *possible* set, surely. For otherwise the story would be literally inconceivable and unimaginable and meaningless.

SOCRATES: I reserve judgment on the issue at least until you finish your fairy tale. It certainly *seems* impossible.

KIERKEGAARD: Why?

SOCRATES: Because, as you said earlier, the God is perfect, and therefore his love is perfect love, which you called *agape*, gift-love instead of need-love. For a God has no needs.

KIERKEGAARD: That is exactly the argument I refute next. Your premise is true but your conclusion does not follow. Men sometimes think that this might be a matter of indifference to the God, since he does not stand in need of the learner. But in this we forget—or rather, alas! We prove how far we are from understanding him; we forget that God loves the learner.

SOCRATES: Such a simple point! How could I have forgotten it? When you said "we forget," in that tiny moment between "forget" and your next words, which tell us *what* it is that we forget, I quickly tested myself, and asked myself just *what* I may have forgotten. And your simple and obvious answer—that it was *that God loves the learner*—this point was *not* among my answers. I always knew I was a fool—that was my only claim to wisdom—but perhaps I was an even greater fool than I realized.

KIERKEGAARD: Welcome to the human race, Socrates. May I continue now?

SOCRATES: Yes. Now that we have established our equality with each other in foolishness, let us explore how the God will solve His problem of establishing equality with us in love.

KIERKEGAARD: It is a real problem for him And just as that kingly grief of which we have spoken can be found only in a kingly soul, and is not even named in the language of the multitude of men, so the entire human language is so selfish that it refuses even to suspect the existence of such a grief. But for that reason the God has reserved it to himself, this unfathomable grief: to know that he may repel the learner, that he does not need him, that the learner has brought destruction upon

}114{

himself by his own guilt, that he can leave the learner to his fate; to know also how well-nigh impossible it is to keep the learner's courage and confidence alive, without which the purposed understanding and equality will fail, and the love become unhappy. The man who cannot feel at least some faint intimation of this grief is a paltry soul of base coinage, bearing neither the image of Caesar nor the image of God.

SOCRATES: I thank you for that compliment. For even though I neither claim to believe nor even to understand this God of yours, I can feel the anguish in His love.

KIERKEGAARD: That proves that you are not merely a philosopher but also a poet. And it is the poet rather than the philosopher whom I invoke here to explore this problem. Thus I next say: **Our problem is now before us, and we invite the poet. . . . The poet's task will be to find a solution, some point of union, where love's understanding may be realized in truth.**

SOCRATES: Of course you realize, even before you begin, that this attempt to solve the God's problem for him will not solve my problem for me. For though I love poets and even am one myself, and not *merely* a philosopher, yet the poet offers no argument to the mind for the truth of his poem, but only the appeal to the imagination based on its beauty.

KIERKEGAARD: I disagree. Beauty can be a servant of truth.

SOCRATES: Of course. But only if truth is known first, so that we know *which* beauties to open our souls to: true ones or deceptive ones.

KIERKEGAARD: Again I disagree. You showed yourself

deeply sensitive to the power of the unconscious mind in the "Meno," where you spoke of "remembering" the Ideas we had forgotten. One of the things this unconscious mind may "remember" is the union between truth and beauty in the greatest poems. And therefore our perception of the deep beauty of a poem may be at last a clue to its truth. But beauty is always perceived *before* truth, for the heart cannot resist the immediate appeal of beauty, but the mind takes much more time to find the truth because the mind has a little guard, a censor, at its gate, and it demands proof, or at least argument, or at least evidence, before it will let the guest through, even though the guest wears the clothes of truth. For the mind knows that clothing can be a deceptive disguise.

SOCRATES: I said something somewhat similar to that in my "Symposium," so I cannot wholly disagree. Yet the heart, or the creative imagination, if you like, is the poet, and the poet is a *maker,* an inventor—the very word "poesis" says that—while the mind is a discoverer. This is why the mind must still judge the heart and the imagination.

KIERKEGAARD: But what of the God? Is He not poet rather than philosopher? Surely He does not seek and discover a wisdom that transcends Him.

SOCRATES: Of course. He would not be a God if He did.

KIERKEGAARD: Then would it not be reasonable to suppose that He would make a poem that is very beautiful?

SOCRATES: Indeed.

KIERKEGAARD: And might He not insert this poem

into time and history so that we His readers could appreciate it and revel in it?

SOCRATES: Certainly.

KIERKEGAARD: And that appreciation and reveling— would not that be a work of the poet in us, of the heart and the imagination rather than the reason?

SOCRATES: That is also true. But just because you find this beauty, that does not mean you find the God. A beautiful poem need not be the work of a God. There were beautiful poems in my culture too—the myths as told by Hesiod and Homer—but they were all works of the human imagination.

KIERKEGAARD: Are you sure of that?

SOCRATES: Yes, for these poems all contained lies, and the God does not lie.

KIERKEGAARD: Might these poems not have been corruptions of an earlier knowledge of the true God, and thus divinely inspired poems overlaid by many gross human layers of error? Is that impossible?

SOCRATES: No. But we must discriminate among the poems, and that is the role of the reason. We cannot simply believe any beautiful poem we hear just because it is beautiful.

KIERKEGAARD: True. But might not the hearing of the poem—I mean what happens in us when we hear it—be a clue as to whether it came from God or man?

SOCRATES: What do you mean by "what happens in us when we hear it"?

KIERKEGAARD: Do you not rank your myths as more

true or false, profounder or shallower, more or less enlightening, by the depth of your immediate response to them? For instance, does not something in your soul immediately and instinctively say "this is silly and shallow" to some of the grosser stories in Ovid's "Metamorphoses" such as a bored and randy god disguising himself as a goat in order to seduce an innocent human woman?

SOCRATES: Yes.

KIERKEGAARD: And does not this same heart of yours leap up with a kind of holy joy when it hears a higher myth such as the love between Amor and Psyche, the god of love and the innocent human soul, which is a purer version of the same story?

SOCRATES: Yes, I think it does. But that does not prove the story is true. For our instinctive responses to poems is hardly an infallible standard. We are fools, and we may very well be deceived by lying but beautiful poems, at least as easily as we are deceived by sophistic but clever philosophies.

KIERKEGAARD: That is true. But might there not be some clues to the truth of a poem that we can find in our very instinctive response to them? For that response is data too, and like all data it may signify something, it may be significant, if we can follow these signs.

You shake your head in doubt and suspicion, Socrates. But is it not possible in theory?

SOCRATES: I suppose so. Why do you pursue this line of questioning? Is that what you plan to do now? To argue for the truth of your poem, or sacred story, or myth, by appealing to my instinctive aesthetic response to it? By arguing that such a moving and beautiful story could not possibly have come from a man, but only from a God?

KIERKEGAARD: Yes, that is indeed my strategy—but with two crucial corrections. First, it is not *my* story. And second, I will not *argue* for its truth, if by "argue" you mean "attempt to prove." I will merely ask a question, in the Socratic style.

SOCRATES: As a poet or as a philosopher?

KIERKEGAARD: Both, at once. For in the very telling of the poem, the story, I will philosophize, I will present the story dialectically, by analyzing the possibilities— either this or that—thus I will combine philosophy with poetry. For the story is about the most poetic of all things, love. So I will do only what you yourself did in the "Symposium."

SOCRATES: Well, then, poeticize away.

9.
The Gospel as Fairy Tale, Continued

KIERKEGAARD: Let me first explain my strategy. It is inherent in my simple division of the story into two stories, "A" and "B." I begin with possibility "A," which is like hypothesis "A" in my earlier chapter. There, "A" was the answer you and your high pagan culture (whether Platonic or Pythagorean or even Hindu or Buddhist) gave to the philosophical question of how we learn the Truth. And "B" was my Christian alternative. So here: "A" will be your pagan version of the sacred story of how a love-union between God and man could be attained, while "B" will be my Christian alternative.

SOCRATES: Thank you for explaining what you will do before you do it. Will you also explain what you have done after you have done it?

KIERKEGAARD: Probably. That is the strategy behind the three-point sermon.

SOCRATES: The *what?*

KIERKEGAARD: It is not important. A cultural artifact in my day. Here is my poem, then:

A.

The union might be brought about by an elevation of the learner. The God would then take him up unto

himself, transfigure him, fill his cup with millennial joys (for a thousand years are as one day in his sight), and let the learner forget the misunderstanding in tumultuous joy.

SOCRATES: This is a familiar story. It happened to many of the heroes in our culture's mythology, for instance "Oedipus at Colonus," the sequel to the most famous play in the world. But I sense that you see a problem with that solution, since you label it "A" to contrast it with your strange alternative, "B." So what is the problem with sacred story "A"?

KIERKEGAARD: Alas, the learner might perhaps be greatly inclined to prize such happiness as this. How wonderful suddenly to find his fortune made, like the humble maiden, because the eye of the God happened to rest upon him! . . . (But) the noble king could perceive the difficulty of such a method, for he was not without insight into the human heart, and understood that the maiden was at bottom deceived; and no one is so terribly deceived as he who does not himself suspect it, but is as if enchanted by a change in the outward habiliments of his existence.[1]

---

1   The attentive and thoughtful reader will perhaps perceive here a theological problem that SK never directly grappled with. SK was a Lutheran, but SK's principles here refute the Lutheran theology of justification and prove the Baptist or even the Catholic one instead. For the God's demand for total truth and not deception would invalidate the Lutheran "federal" theology of justification by legal divine fiat rather than personal ontological transformation (the "new birth"), and perhaps, if thought through to their logical conclusion, would even demand some sort of Purgatory rather than instant glorification.

The union might be brought about by the God's showing himself to the learner and receiving his worship, causing him to forget about himself over the divine apparition. Thus the king might have shown himself to the humble maiden in all the pomp of his power, causing the sun of his presence to rise over her cottage, shedding a glory over the scene and making her forget herself in worshipful admiration. Alas, this might have satisfied the maiden but it could not satisfy the king, who desired not his own glorification but hers.

SOCRATES: Ah! I think I see.

KIERKEGAARD: What do you think you see?

SOCRATES: Why a God who could perform daily miracles does not do so and thereby convince and convert all the unbelievers in the world at once. Because He "desired not His own glorification but hers." A simple and obvious point, like your previous one when you said, "Alas, we forget—that the God *loves* the maiden."

KIERKEGAARD: Yes. It was this that made his grief so hard to bear, his grief that she could not understand him; but it would have been still harder for him to deceive her. And merely to give his love for her an imperfect expression was in his eyes a deception . . .

Not in this manner then can their love be made happy, except perhaps in appearance, namely the learner's and the maiden's, but not the Teacher's and the king's, whom no delusion can satisfy. Thus the God takes pleasure in arraying the lily in a garb more glorious than that of Solomon; but if there could be any thought of an understanding here, would it not be a sorry delusion of the lily's, if when it looked upon its fine raiment it thought that it was on account of the raiment that the God loved it? . . .

There once lived a people who had a profound understanding of the divine; this people thought that no man could see the God and live. Who grasps this contradiction of sorrow: not to reveal oneself is the death of love, to reveal oneself is the death of the beloved!

SOCRATES: That is indeed a profound understanding. And a rare one! For if it is not true, if we can easily see the God and live, then there is no serious problem at all for the God, any more than there was for the gods of my culture. For none of them had such beauty that we would simply die in their presence, as the moth dies in the fire. Who is this people? I assume you are one of them.

KIERKEGAARD: They are the Jews, and we Christians learned who the true God is from them, to whom alone He revealed Himself without error.

SOCRATES: A very large claim, and one I would think is impossible to prove.

B.

KIERKEGAARD: Impossible to prove, perhaps, but not impossible to believe. But let me go on with my story. I now proceed to alternative "B."

The union must therefore be brought about in some other way. . . . Since we found that the union could not be brought about by an elevation it must be attempted by a descent.

SOCRATES: I had thought religion was man's search for God. You are proposing that it is the God's search for man.

KIERKEGAARD: Yes.

SOCRATES: It would follow, then, that to speak of religion as "man's search for God" is rather like speaking of the bone's search for the dog.

KIERKEGAARD: Something like that would follow, yes.

SOCRATES: How very strange.

KIERKEGAARD: This very strangeness, this surprisingness—do you see it as evidence *against* the truth of the story?

SOCRATES: You speak as if you considered it evidence *for* it. But how can that be? Do you say that the more ridiculous a story seems, the more likely it is to be true? Do you want to say "I believe because it is absurd"?

KIERKEGAARD: Actually, there was a famous Christian who did say exactly that. His name was Tertullian. But he was a heretic. No, I do not quite want to say that. Nor do I want to say of stories that the more ridiculous they are the more likely they are. That is obviously not true of stories in general. But this story is not about man but about God. And so if it did *not* appear to us as surprising, even astonishing, and perhaps even ridiculous at first, we would be justified in suspecting that we had only made it up ourselves. For we are not surprised by our own minds, but only by minds that are very different than ours, and usually by minds that are superior to ours, and by the products of such minds. Is this not so?

SOCRATES: It is indeed so. My mind is like my house, open for strange visitors at any time. Proceed.

KIERKEGAARD: Let the learner be *x*. In this *x* we must include the lowliest; for if even Socrates refused to establish a false fellowship with the clever, how can we suppose that the God would make a distinction?

SOCRATES: I wish to register a strong protest against being used as any kind of a touchstone for what the God would do!

KIERKEGAARD: Protest noted. But that is not what I meant. My argument was an *a fortiori*: if even a mere man like you did not discriminate, how much less would the perfect God do so?

SOCRATES: Correction accepted. Please proceed.

KIERKEGAARD: In order that the union may be brought about, the God must therefore become the equal of such a one, and so he will appear in the likeness of the humblest. But the humblest is one who must serve others, and the God will therefore appear in the form of a *servant.*

SOCRATES: A strange conclusion, but it logically follows from our premises.

KIERKEGAARD: But this servant-form is no mere outer garment, like the king's beggar-cloak. . . . It is his true form and figure. For this is the unfathomable nature of love, that it desires equality with the beloved, not in jest merely, but in earnest and truth . . .

SOCRATES: What an exceedingly strange kind of love for a God to have! If I have any idea of what a real God must be, as distinct from the pitiful figures my mythology invented, then this love of His would be not merely like a king desiring to marry a servant girl but almost like a man desiring to marry an insect!

KIERKEGAARD: And the only way to do that would be first to *become* an insect. You are right three times, Socrates—right about the great difference between the true God and man, and right about what the God would do to overcome this difference, and right about the surpassing strangeness of His love that would move Him to do this.

SOCRATES: In that case I must tell you that I find your story almost unbelievable.

KIERKEGAARD: "Almost" is "not quite," I hope.

SOCRATES: Well, not yet, at least. Let us go on.

KIERKEGAARD: Behold where he stands—the God! Where? There; do you not see him? He is the God; and yet he has not a resting-place for his head, and he dares not to lean on any man lest he cause him to be offended. He is the God; and yet he picks his steps more carefully than if angels guided them, not to prevent his foot from stumbling against a stone, but lest he trample human beings in the dust, in that they are offended in him . . .

To sustain the heavens and the earth by the fiat of his omnipotent word, so that if this word were withdrawn for the fraction of a second the universe would be plunged into chaos—how light a task compared with bearing the burden that mankind may take offense, when one has been constrained by love to become its savior!

But the servant-form is no mere outer garment, and therefore the God must suffer all things, endure all things, make experience of all things. He must suffer hunger in the desert, he must thirst in the time of his agony, he must be forsaken in death, absolutely like the humblest—behold the man! His suffering is not (only) that of his death, but this entire life is a story of suffering; and it is love that suffers. The love that gives all is itself in want. What wonderful self-denial! For though the learner be one of the lowliest, he nevertheless asks him anxiously, Do you now really love me? For he knows where the danger threatens, and yet he also knows that every easier way would involve a deception, even though the learner might not understand it.

SOCRATES: But if the God is omnipotent, why does he not simply change the learner into a saint that could understand and endure his love?

KIERKEGAARD: Because the God is love, and **love does not alter the beloved, it alters itself.**

SOCRATES: So the God is altered by love?

KIERKEGAARD: No, he alters himself. He *is* love.

SOCRATES: But he changes.

KIERKEGAARD: Yes.

SOCRATES: He is subject, then, to passion, and passivity? He falls in love, as a man does?

KIERKEGAARD: No. A dry man falls into the sea and gets wet. But the sea does not fall into the sea or get wet. We fall into and out of love; the God *is* love.

SOCRATES: As a sort of Platonic Form?

KIERKEGAARD: No. As a sort of volcano.

SOCRATES: I think I understand only one thing about this God of yours: that I understand nothing about him.

KIERKEGAARD: An auspicious beginning!—if we are to take your "learned ignorance" seriously.

SOCRATES: Touché!

KIERKEGAARD: So because every other form of revelation would be a deception from the standpoint of divine love . . . , therefore if I asked him to alter his purpose, to reveal himself differently, to be more lenient with himself, he would doubtless look at me and say: Man, what have I to do with thee? Get thee hence, for thou art Satan, though thou knowest it not! . . . I would doubtless see him weep also over me, and hear him say: To think that you could prove so faithless, and so wound my love! Is it then only the omnipotent wonder-worker that you love, and not him who humbled himself to become your equal?

But the servant-form was no mere outer garment; hence he must yield his spirit in death and again leave the earth . . . if I begged him to save his life and stay upon the earth, it would only be to see him sorrowful unto death, and stricken with grief also for my sake, because this suffering was for my profit, and now I had added to his sorrow the burden that I could not understand him. O bitter cup! More bitter than wormwood is the bitterness of death for a mortal, how bitter then for an immortal!

SOCRATES: How are we supposed to react to this? Is it a mere spectacle to dazzle us and confuse us?

KIERKEGAARD: Indeed not.

SOCRATES: What, then, is to happen to us?

KIERKEGAARD: We are transformed into the likeness of the God, that is, into love. As I say next, **And now** the learner, has he no lot or part in this story of suffering, even though his lot cannot be that of the Teacher? Aye, it cannot be otherwise. And the cause of all this suffering is love, precisely because the God is not jealous for himself, but desires in love to be the equal of the humblest. When the seed of the oak is planted in earthen vessels, they break asunder; when new wine is poured in old leathern bottles, they burst; what must happen when the God implants himself in human weakness, unless man becomes a new vessel and a new creature! But this becoming, what labors will attend the change, how convulsed with birth-pangs!

SOCRATES: Why must there be "birth-pangs"?

KIERKEGAARD: Because the God does more than save us from loneliness and lovelessness and guilt and punishment for our sins. He was called "Savior" not because he would save us from all these *effects* of our sins, but because he would save us from our *sins*.

SOCRATES: I do not see how the story can be true; and yet it makes my spirit tremble.

KIERKEGAARD: That is not surprising. For it is indeed less terrible to fall to the ground when the mountains tremble at the voice of God, than to sit at table with him as an equal; and yet it is the God's concern precisely to have it so.

10.
The Argument: Reasons to Believe the "Fairy Tale"

SOCRATES: But you . . . you seem an intelligent fellow. How can you bring yourself to believe such a story? Is such belief a sheer leap in the dark?

KIERKEGAARD: It is indeed a leap, but not in the dark.

SOCRATES: You have reasons, then, for believing it.

KIERKEGAARD: Yes, though not the kind of reasons you are probably thinking of.

SOCRATES: I think you can guess what my next question will be.

KIERKEGAARD: What are those reasons, and what kind of reasons are they?

SOCRATES: Exactly.

KIERKEGAARD: I will answer the first of those two questions, and you will see for yourself, in examining my reasons, what kind of reasons they are.

SOCRATES: Go ahead, then.

KIERKEGAARD: I begin my argument with an objection.

SOCRATES: A strange way to begin an argument. For if the thing you are arguing for is true, all objections against it are erroneous. Why begin with the erroneous?

KIERKEGAARD: Because it is *not* erroneous. The objection is true. But it is not an objection against the *truth* of my story, but against the supposition that it is *my* story.

SOCRATES: Ah, I see your strategy. It is the same strategy you used at the end of your first chapter, when we treated your religion as a philosophy instead of a fairy tale. Go on, then, please.

KIERKEGAARD: (1) Now if someone were to say: "This poem of yours is the most wretched piece of plagiarism ever perpetrated, for it is neither more nor less than what every child (in Christendom) knows," I suppose I must blush with shame to hear myself called a liar. But why the most wretched? Every poet who steals, steals from some other poet, and in so far we are all equally wretched; indeed, my own theft is perhaps less harmful, since it is more readily discovered. If I were to be so polite as to ascribe the authorship to you who now condemn me, you would perhaps again be angry. Is there then no poet, although there is a poem? This would be strange, as strange as flute-playing without a flute-player.

(2) Or is this poem perhaps like a proverb, for which no author can be assigned because it is as if it owed its existence to humanity at large. Was this perhaps the reason you called my theft the most wretched, because I did not steal from any individual man but robbed the human race, and arrogantly, although I am only an individual man, aye, even a wretched thief,

pretended to be mankind? If this then is the case, and I went about to all men in turn, and all knew the poem but each one also knew that he was not the author of it, can I then conclude: mankind must be the author? Would this not be a strange conclusion? For if mankind were the author of the poem, this would have to be expressed by considering every individual equally close to the authorship.

(3) Does it not seem to you that this is a difficult case in which we have become involved, though the whole matter appeared to be so easily disposed of in the beginning, by your short and angry word about its being the most wretched plagiarism, and my shame in having to hear it? So then perhaps it is no poem, or at any rate not one for which any human being is responsible, nor yet mankind; ah, now I understand you, it was for this reason you called my procedure the most wretched act of plagiarism, because I did not steal from any individual, nor from the race, but from the God. . . . Now I understand you fully, dear friend, and recognize the justice of your resentment.

But then my soul is filled with new wonder, even more, with the spirit of worship; for it would surely have been strange had this poem been a human production. It is not impossible that it might occur to man to imagine himself the equal of the God, or to imagine the God the equal of man, but not to imagine that the God would make himself into the likeness of man; for if the God gave no sign, how could it enter into the mind of man that the blessed God should need him? This would be a most stupid thought, or rather, so stupid a thought could never have entered into his mind; though when the God has seen fit to entrust him with it he exclaims in worship: This thought did not arise in my own heart! and finds it a most miraculously beautiful thought.

And is it not altogether miraculous? And does not this word come as a happy omen to my lips? For as I have just said, and as you yourself involuntarily exclaim, we stand here before the *Miracle*. And as we both now stand before this miracle, whose solemn silence cannot be perturbed by human wrangling over mine and thine, whose awe-inspiring speech infinitely subdues all human strife about mine and thine, forgive me, I pray, the strange delusion that I was the author of this poem. It was a delusion, and the poem is so different from every human poem as not to be a poem at all, but the *Miracle*.

SOCRATES: Your rhetoric is beautiful, but I sense there is also an argument in it. And since I trust arguments more than rhetoric, I wonder if I could trouble you to extract the argument from the rhetoric, as one would extract the bones from the carcass of a chicken. Most people prefer to eat the flesh of the chicken, but I would prefer to inspect the bones.

KIERKEGAARD: You are a strange bird yourself, Socrates. But not so strange; most philosophers are like that. But most philosophers do not have also a sense of poetry, and a love of it, as you do. So I have hope that the two halves of your soul may meet and agree about this story. But for that to happen, we must, as you say, extract the bones from the chicken and examine them. I will honor your request, therefore, to subject this poem that I have called "the Miracle" to a logical examination.

The long passage that I just read is not part of the sacred story itself, but distances itself from the story and looks at the story with a detached and logical attitude, just as *you* habitually did. It is ironic in tone, but it contains a serious logical argument. The argument is based on the commonsensical principle of causality: that nothing can come into existence without an adequate cause; that there cannot be more in the effect that in its cause or causes. I then offer a disjunctive syllogism, an "either/or" argument that offers three possible causes for the effect, three possible origins of this story. (This is why I have labeled the first three parts of this long paragraph "(1)," "(2)," and "(3).") If there is a poem, there must be a poet, by the principle of causality. Poems do not just happen, nor do they happen because of anything less than a poet—for instance, throwing an ink-filled pen at an empty paper. The first possible cause is myself as the poet. The second is any other human being as the poet, or the whole human race together. And the third is no human being at all, but the God. If the first two possible causes can be eliminated, only the third one remains.

SOCRATES: So you think you can prove that this story comes from the God by this argument?

KIERKEGAARD: No, I do not say it is a *proof*, for a valid logical proof leaves no room for free choice. But the whole point of the story fails if mankind has no free choice over against the God. That was one of the problems with story "A," after all. I do say, though, that even though it is not a *proof*, it is a powerful *clue*, like a fingerprint—a clue powerful enough to convict the conscience of its hearer of error if the hearer rises up in instinctive rebellion and resentment against the story.

The one who first *lived* this story that others then told—the God who came into time—always elicited one of two reactions from everyone who ever met him: either hate or love, rebellion or discipleship, outrage or worship. Both reactions were forms of wonder, astonishment, or amazement. All four writers of the Gospels, the four accounts of his life that we have, constantly use the Greek word *thaumadzein* for both reactions to him: the reaction of his disciples, who instinctively loved him and gradually learned to believe him and trust him, and the reaction of his enemies, who instinctively hated and feared him and sought to kill him.

SOCRATES: I think if I met him I would have had a third reaction: puzzlement. And this is *another* form of wonder, or *thaumadzein*. But that is neither the judgment that He is to be worshipped nor the judgment that He is to be executed, but it is a suspension of judgment. I have this habit, you see, of wanting adequate reasons for either loving or hating a man or a story.

KIERKEGAARD: I should have mentioned your third alternative too, Socrates. For there were many in his day who met him and embraced that alternative, which we may call the agnostic one. They went away shaking their heads, muttering "No man ever spoke like this man," and not knowing whether to become his friends or his enemies. But these people knew that eventually they would have to become one or the other.

The point of my defining these three reactions to the story is to help you play the prophet to yourself. The story, like the divine storyteller, always works like a mirror: it reveals the hidden face of the one who hears it. Many have an initial, instinctive reaction of opposition and even fear, a hidden *wish* that it be not true. Others have an initial reaction of fascination and a wish that it be true.

SOCRATES: Are there none who have neither reaction?

KIERKEGAARD: Yes. Some are simply bored by it and do not care whether it is true or false. And these are the farthest of all from the truth of the story. For if you hate a man, you at least acknowledge his importance, and are closer to loving him than if you are bored by him. A vehicle traveling at great speed in the wrong direction can be converted, that is, turned around, more easily than one that is unmoving and stuck in the mud.

SOCRATES: But a man like me must have reasons for this turning round, or conversion. That was the word I used for the prisoner's exit from the cave in my famous parable that Plato put into his "Republic." There are actually three conversions in this story. First, there is a conversion when the freed prisoner chooses to turn his neck to see the truer realities behind him rather than just the habitual shadows in front of him on the wall of the cave. The bored would not even do that, I think. And there is a second conversion when he turns his body and moves his legs to follow these higher lights and to struggle out of the cave. Finally, when he escapes into the outside world and stands in the new, strange light of the sun in this far larger world, his eyes need time to convert to a new mode of seeing. I suspect that all three conversions are necessary in your story too. Is this not so?

KIERKEGAARD: It is so.

SOCRATES: And so you cannot expect an instant conversion from me. You can expect only the first of the three conversions, the initial curiosity and interest, and even fascination. And this conversion you have indeed accomplished in my soul. But the other two, the climbing into the new kind of light and the accustoming the eyes to it—this, it seems to me, must always be a process that takes time—sometimes a short time, sometimes a long time—if the conversion is authentic and if it is to take root in the soul.

KIERKEGAARD: Indeed. In fact all of life is a process of *becoming* that which one is. But I think the seed has taken root in your soul, Socrates. And I think it will grow very quickly.

11.
Three Answers to
Life's Central Question

KIERKEGAARD: It seems I was right about one thing, at least, in my philosophy, and that was the thing that pervaded every sentence I ever wrote.

SOCRATES: What is that?

KIERKEGAARD: That there are three basic answers to life's central question, three "stages on life's way."

SOCRATES: You realize that to call them three stages on a single way presupposes something, assumes something, do you not?

KIERKEGAARD: Yes. It presupposes a unity and a plan to life's way. It assumes that there are stages of growth designed to move us in a single direction as we mature.

SOCRATES: What justifies that assumption?

KIERKEGAARD: Not argument but experience. The experience of the vast variety of human lives and the patterns that emerge from looking at them. I called them "the aesthetic," "the ethical," and "the religions" ways of life, or modes of human existence. Do you understand these three patterns, Socrates? I think you do.

SOCRATES: From my encounter with philosophers like Freud, I think I understand the first two, theirs and mine. But until our conversation today, I thought there were only those two options: materialism and spiritualism, pessimism and optimism, immoralism and moralism, the animal and the rational, the goods of the body and the goods of the soul.

KIERKEGAARD: What about religion?

SOCRATES: I classified religion as part of the second answer.

KIERKEGAARD: Why do you question that now?

SOCRATES: Because you have spoken of a different kind of religion than any I ever knew, and you have made a good case for its being a fundamentally different option for human existence.

KIERKEGAARD: So how do you see the options now?

SOCRATES: I see three possible fundamental answers, rather than two, to life's greatest question.

KIERKEGAARD: And that great question is. . . ?

SOCRATES: It is the question of "the meaning of life," or the highest end and purpose of life, the "greatest good" or "summum bonum."

KIERKEGAARD: And the three possible answers?

SOCRATES: They are (1) to touch a body in animal lust, (2) to touch eternal truth in human intelligence, or (3) to *be* touched by the love of God in the heart.

KIERKEGAARD: That is indeed a way to summarize my three "stages": for the body to be touched by

SOCRATES MEETS KIERKEGAARD

sensual pleasure, for the soul to be touched by eternal truth, or for the spirit to be touched by divine love.

SOCRATES: They are also three possible *relationships*: with what is less than ourselves, with ourselves, or at least our minds, and with what is more than ourselves; in other words, with the world, with the self, or with God. Is this not so?

KIERKEGAARD: Yes. That is why each is a quantum leap over the other; different in kind, not just in degree.

SOCRATES: I suspect that not only are their *objects* different—world, self, or God—but also the *quality* of the good, or the *kind* of good that is sought in each stage. I even wonder whether we should use the same word, "happiness," for all three. For I discovered, in conversing with Freud, that some people mean something so different by "happiness" than others mean—in his case, the most intense bodily pleasure, sexual orgasm; in my case the perfection of soul brought about by possessing and practicing the intellectual and moral virtues—that it is very misleading to use the same word for both. Do you agree?

KIERKEGAARD: I do. Perhaps we should use the word "pleasure" for the aesthetic end, "happiness" (*eudaimonia*) for your ethical and intellectual end, and "joy" for the religious end. These too are different in kind, not just in degree.

SOCRATES: You probably know what I am going to ask for next. I cannot think well without definitions.

KIERKEGAARD: Would a clear distinction between them satisfy you, without a formal logical *definition* of each one, with genus and specific difference?

SOCRATES: If it has to suffice, it has to suffice.

KIERKEGAARD: Then let us say that *happiness*—at least as you and Plato and Aristotle and your many followers conceived it—is not just a deeper kind of *pleasure*, one that is inward and spiritual rather than outward and material, but it is the moral and intellectual perfection of one's character. It is an objective state, not a subjective feeling. It is so far from being a form of pleasure that it is not only compatible with suffering, the very opposite of pleasure, but it thrives only when there *is* suffering to make it wise.

SOCRATES: That is clear. But what is this third thing, which you called "joy"? How is that different from happiness?

KIERKEGAARD: For one thing, its cause, or condition, is not virtue but faith.

SOCRATES: So it can come even to the foolish and wicked?

KIERKEGAARD: Yes, Socrates. That is the only reason there is hope for fools like us.

SOCRATES: Why is it not just a deeper kind of happiness?

KIERKEGAARD: Because it is not *contentment*, not the satisfaction of a previously known and felt desire, but a surprise, a gift, a grace.

SOCRATES: So it is not under our control?

KIERKEGAARD: No. Happiness is under our control. As you pointed out in many of your dialogs, we are responsible for our own happiness, for we are responsible for our own virtue, and virtue is the key to happiness. But the cause of our joy is not ourselves. It is God.

SOCRATES: Is that why faith is necessary?

KIERKEGAARD: Yes. Faith is saying Yes to the gift, like accepting a marriage proposal. Remember my parable of the king and the humble maiden.

SOCRATES: I see. And I think I see that the choice is also a metaphysical one, a choice about what is ultimately *real*.

KIERKEGAARD: How?

SOCRATES: The aesthetic way implies both atheism and materialism. My rational-moral way implies the superior reality of the soul and an absolute good, a kind of God without a face. And your religious way implies that the God is a person and is perfect love.

KIERKEGAARD: This is true.

SOCRATES: It is also a choice of anthropologies, of answers to "know thyself."

KIERKEGAARD: How do you see that?

SOCRATES: For one who is on the first stage of life, like Freud, or Hobbes, or Marx, or Machiavelli, we are only intelligent animals. For me, we are rational souls. For you, we are God's beloved children. Each anthropology is a quantum leap from the others.

KIERKEGAARD: The category I use for the third is "spirit." I distinguish three aspects of ourselves, parallel to the three stages. Where you distinguished only body and soul, Socrates, I distinguish body, soul and spirit. With the body we relate to what is less than ourselves, to the material world, the universe, because your body is not only a part of yourself but also a part of the world. We relate to other people as ingredients in that world, as objects. With the soul we relate to ourselves and other subjects like us. With the spirit, we relate to God, who is infinitely above us.

SOCRATES: So God is *infinite?* Is it possible for the finite to relate to the infinite? Or to conceive it, in any way? We Greeks tended to see infinity as an imperfection rather than a perfection, you know.

KIERKEGAARD: But you yourself broke that Greek mold at least twice. One was in the "Republic" when you spoke of the supreme reality, the supreme good and the supreme Idea, the Idea of the Good, as "infinite." Your disciples were astonished. And the other was in the "Symposium" when you spoke of the absolute Beauty. You called it an "infinite ocean of beauty."

SOCRATES: I did say that, though I barely understood the tiniest part of what I was saying.

KIERKEGAARD: Most of us are in that position most of the time, I think, once we stop fooling ourselves.

SOCRATES: I see you have learned my Lesson One about wisdom being the knowledge of our own ignorance. Can you tell me what you mean by "spirit," then? Is it our ability as finite creatures to relate to the infinite God? Is that what distinguishes what you mean by "spirit" from what you mean by "soul"?

KIERKEGAARD: Yes. I call us "spirit" because we are related to the Absolute Spirit.

SOCRATES: That relationship sounds perilously

fragile—something reserved for those few mountain climbers who can exist in airless and freezing heights.

KIERKEGAARD: Not at all. This relationship is not an unusual achievement of our own but written into our very being by our Creator.

SOCRATES: So this relationship to God is not accidental but essential to our very being.

KIERKEGAARD: Yes.

SOCRATES: So if we lose it, we lose both God and ourselves.

KIERKEGAARD: Yes.

SOCRATES: Nothing could be more necessary, then, and more practical, than discovering whether both of these two things are true: this God and this self. These are the only two things worth finding, in the end.

KIERKEGAARD: Yes. Our divine teacher once made that point in the most practical sentence any man ever spoke: "What does it profit a man if he gain the whole world and lose his own self?"

SOCRATES: So this is life's supreme choice.

KIERKEGAARD: Precisely. And therefore *your* supreme choice. How then will you choose among these three, Socrates? Will it be the "pleasure principle" for your body, the harmony of happiness for your soul, or the joy of Jesus for your spirit?

12.
The Decision:
What Would Socrates Believe?

KIERKEGAARD: Where do you think you will go from here, Socrates? Can you forecast your future from your present state of mind?

SOCRATES: My first reaction would be to compare the lucid self-evidence of my philosophy of reason and virtue with the strange, nearly unbelievable paradox of your Christian story. But, then, sometimes a thick and murky soup is more nourishing than a thin and clear one. And there is one question about your story that I cannot help seeing as a strange but powerful clue to its truth. That is the question of the origin of it, the origin of the idea of the God in love with man.

You have two arguments here, I think. First, you present your three possible answers to this question and argue for the third one—that the God is the cause of the poem—by eliminating the other two—that either you or all of mankind is the cause.

Then you present a second argument, which is a more psychological one rather than a strictly logical one. You say:

But then my soul is filled with new wonder, even more, with the spirit of worship; for it would surely

have been strange had this poem been a human production. It is not impossible that it might occur to man to
imagine himself the equal of the God, or to imagine the
God the equal of man, but not to imagine that the God
would make himself into the likeness of man; for if the
God gave no sign, how could it enter into the mind of
man that the blessed God should need him? This would
be a most stupid thought, or rather, so stupid a thought
could never have entered into his mind; though when
the God has seen fit to entrust him with it he exclaims
in worship: This thought did not arise in my own heart!
and finds it a most miraculously beautiful thought.

The argument is *almost* that the story is so ridiculous that it must be true; that it must be believed
because it is absurd. If anyone presented this argument
without any content to the "it" that we were arguing
about, I would instantly say that this was the most idi-
otic of all possible arguments.

KIERKEGAARD: But that is not your final and complete verdict on the subject?

SOCRATES: No, for when I fill in this "it" with the
content of your sacred story, then I find that its very
paradoxicality can be seen as an argument *for* it. For a
paradox is an *apparent* contradiction, but not a real
one, and in many areas of life the surprising, the astonishing, and the paradoxical are precisely the truth.
Reality is seldom what we first imagine and expect; and
therefore if a story *is* exactly what we imagine and
expect, and everyone easily accepts it because it matches their expectations, that is a reason for suspecting the
story is *not* true. This is true of the nature of the physical world, but it is also true of friendship: the reason
friendship is one of the few things in life that escape

boredom is that even the closest friends constantly surprise each other with new revelations about themselves.

KIERKEGAARD: So how do you evaluate my story, then, if your mind tells you such conflicting things about it?

SOCRATES: I don't know what to say about the story itself, but I can say something about the effect the story has upon my soul. The first effect on my soul is a negative one: the story seems to contradict reason—if we identify reason with my philosophy, what you called hypothesis "A." And I simply cannot abandon my reason, for that would be to abandon my honesty, and thus my very self. The story certainly seems not only unreasonable (you yourself call it "the absolute paradox"), but self-contradictory—the ultimate logical sin.

KIERKEGAARD: Why?

SOCRATES: For two reasons. One reason is to be found in each of your two essays, or chapters. First, in your philosophical alternative to my notion of how we learn the Truth, there is this strange and seemingly self-contradictory notion of Eternity acquiring a beginning, the eternal God becoming a temporal man. Then, in your second chapter, there is a parallel paradox: of the God's *agape* adding a human *eros* to itself, I mean the notion of this perfect God, who has no needs, loving us and desiring us.

KIERKEGAARD: Does your reason tell you the nature of this God so clearly that you are sure you could not be wrong about Him?

SOCRATES: Obviously not. And I surely do not know enough about Time, much less about Eternity, to be sure that Eternity cannot possibly add to itself a beginning in Time.

KIERKEGAARD: This is an example of the limitations of our reason, Socrates, when confronted with divine things.

SOCRATES: Do you mean that if there were no such limitation of reason, then Faith could have no place to enter us?

KIERKEGAARD: No, that is not what I mean, for that treats Faith as a competitor with reason, perhaps implying that it is a second-rate substitute for reason in inferior minds. But Faith is more than that. It is not merely what you called "belief" or "right opinion" (in the "Meno"). That would be merely a second-rate substitute for reason, and thus something in the mind.

SOCRATES: What else is it, then?

KIERKEGAARD: I note in one of my Journal entries (Nov. 2, 1834) that **Faith, surely, implies an act of the will . . . how can I otherwise explain the saying in the New Testament** (Romans 14:23) **that whatsoever is not of faith is sin.**

SOCRATES: That saying seems to be a confusion of categories. Though these two things may be closely connected, as I myself taught when I said that all evil stems from ignorance, still the concept of faith, in itself, refers to something intellectual while the concept of sin refers to something moral.

KIERKEGAARD: Not in the new sense of both words in the New Testament. Faith is not just a good thing in epistemology and sin is not just a bad thing in morality.

They are both ontological states, religious states, relational states. Faith is the positive relation to God and sin is the negative one. Faith is the acceptance of the God's love and sin is the rejection of it. They are like the two possible answers to a marriage proposal, or to a seduction.

SOCRATES: If that is so, then they are not matters of degree, since no one can be partly married, or partly pregnant .

KIERKEGAARD: Precisely.

SOCRATES: The more I learn of this strange story of yours, the more I suspect that perhaps it is not as inconsistent as I had thought. But of course a well-made fairy tale is perfectly consistent in itself even if it is not true of the real world. So this may be merely a consistent fairy tale, not the Truth.

You showed the consistency of both my philosophy and yours, which you labeled "A" and "B," point by point in your first essay, or your first chapter, when you compared the two philosophies point by point. And you admitted that my "A" seemed eminently reasonable.

KIERKEGAARD: Since both "A" and "B" are consistent, and thus *possible,* do you find yourself naturally drawn to one more than the other?

SOCRATES: I do.

KIERKEGAARD: To which?

SOCRATES: If you are speaking of being *naturally* drawn, then it is to "A." I can say that because I know something about my own nature. But if you ask me about being *supernaturally* drawn, I must plead igno-rance.

KIERKEGAARD: Why is your nature more drawn to "A"?

SOCRATES: Not just because it is mine. But because "B" seems perilously close to irrationality, impossibili-ty, and self-contradiction. For at the heart of "B," in both of your two chapters, was the story of the eternal God entering time and acquiring a beginning. This seemed to me perilously close to a real contradiction and not just a paradox. How could Eternity get a beginning in time?

KIERKEGAARD: If not, how could the Moment be eternally important?

SOCRATES: But how *could* the Moment in time be eternally important?

KIERKEGAARD: Why could it not be? Do you know enough about time and eternity to be certain of the answer to that question?

SOCRATES: I must admit that I do not. But the second cause of my skepticism came when you turned to your second essay, or second chapter, the story of the God's love. It is a beautiful story, and not without adumbra-tions within my own culture's mythology. It is a story that every good man would wish was true; so even when it had a negative magnetism toward the reason it had a positive magnetism toward the heart.

KIERKEGAARD: So you now find your intelligence and your heart at odds.

SOCRATES: I do. And I cannot believe that the human

soul is so badly constructed that this is its natural or inevitable state. So I am convinced that one of those two parts is functioning wrongly. But I do not know which one it is.

KIERKEGAARD: Can you weigh these two parts, and these two reactions, against each other and choose one over the other?

SOCRATES: No, but when I put them against each other two opposite possibilities emerge. One is the tragic need to choose between them, to betray either my mind or my heart. But the other, which balances it, and puts me on a kind of spiritual seesaw, is the possibility that they are in alliance after all, even in their present condition of apparently contradicting each other. For sometimes the negative is a necessary precondition for the positive; and war can be a precondition for peace. So perhaps the very paradoxicality of the story can make it attractive, not so much to the heart—that attraction was already there—but to the reason. If the God is real, and is infinite love, and does incarnate himself, and is infinitely wiser and trickier than our paltry human minds could predict, then this love, this "incarnation," this strange story might well be His supreme trick, and just the way he *would* act, though no one could predict that, only see it with afterthought.

KIERKEGAARD: Epimetheus has always had stronger sight than Prometheus, after all.

SOCRATES: Quite so. So the upshot of it all is that you have put me in the same position others complained I put them in: confusion, uncertainty, even a kind of fear and trembling, like a swimmer caught between incoming and outgoing tides.

KIERKEGAARD: And if you determined, in the end, that the story is *not* true, what do you think would happen in your soul? Can you give me a kind of inner weather forecast?

SOCRATES: I think that then a great sadness would overcome my soul, and I could never go back to my innocent and reasonable philosophy.

KIERKEGAARD: That is exactly what my weather forecast also predicts.

SOCRATES: I have been told, by the Authorities who prepared me to meet you, that the overall structure and strategy of your entire philosophy, throughout your many books, has been to chart and encourage a progress up the three "stages of life's way," or stages of human existence, the aesthetic, the ethical, and the religious. My philosophy was, for you, the highest expression of the second stage, and you now invite me on a second journey out of a cave, the cave of my own reason, and into a higher light.

Others, like Marx, Machiavelli, Hume, Sartre, and Freud, on the other hand, have told me that even my first escape from the cave was an illusion; that all value is relative and subjective; and that there is no hope of satisfaction for the deepest of all human desires; in fact, that the deeper or higher the desire, the more deceptive it is.

This is my affliction, and you have not comforted the afflicted, you have afflicted the comfortable. You have not converted me, but you have made it impossible for me to remain in my comfortable middle sphere, the ethical-rational. So that I must either move ahead and upwards or down and backwards, either staking everything on a higher hope, however irrational it seems, or sinking back into a deeper despair than even my enemies the Sophists professed. That is what you have proved to me. You have not proved that your religious story is true; it may be no more than "a project of thought" and "an essay of the imagination" But you have shown it to be part of an either/or: not merely the "either/or" of the aesthetic or the ethical, which is the point of your book by that title, but the "either/or" of the aesthetic or the religious. For I cannot now go back to my innocent ethical rationalism. There is a gap behind me now as well as in front of me.

KIERKEGAARD: That is essentially what I myself say on the very last page: **The projected hypothesis indisputably makes an advance upon Socrates, which is apparent at every point. Whether it is therefore more true than the Socratic doctrine is an entirely different question, which cannot be decided in the same breath, since we have here assumed a new organ: Faith; a new presupposition: the consciousness of Sin; a new decision: the Moment; and a new Teacher: the God in Time. Without these I certainly never would have dared present myself for inspection before that master of Irony, admired through the centuries, whom I approach with a palpitating enthusiasm that yields to none. But to make an advance upon Socrates and yet say essentially the same things as he, only not nearly so well—that, at least, is not Socratic.**

SOCRATES: You have indeed been Socratic, Søren. You have played Socrates to Socrates.

KIERKEGAARD: Thank you. I can think of no higher compliment, and from no higher human source.

SOCRATES: But where am I now, as a result? If I reject

your story, it seems I must despair and embrace nihilism, including its nihilism of reason, its suspicion of reason, its reduction of reason to rationalization. And if I embrace your faith and hope, I must uproot my rational and ethical foundation, and anchor it in something else, something even more ultimate, what you call Faith in this God in time. In either case, I cannot simply remain comfortably where I am.

KIERKEGAARD: You are like the protagonist in a famous English novel, "Pride and Prejudice," who is told by her father: "A terrible dilemma is before you, Elizabeth. From this day forth you must be a stranger to one of your parents. Your mother will never speak to you again if you do not marry Mr. Collins and I will not speak to you again if you do."

SOCRATES: I see. So I am like this Elizabeth, and you are like this Mr. Collins, and your proposal of marriage puts me in a position where I must alienate one of my two parents, either my mind or my heart.

KIERKEGAARD: Unless you can get your parents to reconcile, yes. Perhaps some day you will meet a man like Augustine who has done that.

SOCRATES: You have done a dangerous thing, Søren. You have undermined the one stable ground in my life, my confidence that human reason is the court of last appeal, the firmest of foundations, the anchor that secures us in the bedrock of Truth. Embracing your story would give my reason wings, and I would cease to be a mammal with four feet on the ground and become a bird, soaring into the heavens (though it would of course frequently return to earth). Rejecting your story would sink me into despair and turn me into a fish, unable to even breathe the air, much less fly in it.

So you have set me on a road to—well, to what? To the unknown, certainly.

KIERKEGAARD: Perhaps to what you have called "The Miracle."

SOCRATES: Perhaps.

KIERKEGAARD: And perhaps you are in higher hands than your own.

SOCRATES: Fate, you mean?

KIERKEGAARD: No, I mean hands that play the part of Socrates to Socrates.

SOCRATES: Do you mean that in all my questioning, I am *being* questioned by the God?

KIERKEGAARD: That is exactly what I mean.

SOCRATES: If that is so, I wonder where He will send me next.

KIERKEGAARD: He is utterly unpredictable. It could be a place as dangerous as the doors of Hell, or as paradisical as the porches of Heaven, or as confused as the classrooms of Harvard.

Concluding Unscientific Postscript

Well, what next? What next for Socrates? What next for you?

Readers interested in tracing the further adventures of Socrates may peruse *Socrates Meets Jesus* (InterVarsity Press), in which the third of Kierkegaard's above predictions comes true. It's Harvard. Or, in *The Best Things in Life,* Desperate State University.

Socrates also has other encounters with philosophers in the next world:

Socrates Meets Machiavelli
Socrates Meets Marx
Socrates Meets Sartre
Socrates Meets Descartes
Socrates Meets Hume
Socrates Meets Kant
Socrates Meets Freud

Readers who are interested in finding out whether the two parts of Socrates' soul, the mind and the heart, reason and faith, can reconcile like two estranged parents, or fly together like the two wings of a bird, or breathe together the same air of truth, like the two lungs, may explore this question in many of the author's other books, notably

Christianity for Modern Pagans: Pascal's Pensees *Edited and Explained* (Ignatius Press);

Summa of the Summa: the Essential Philosophical Passages of St. Thomas Aquinas' Summa Theologica *Edited and Explained for Beginners* (Ignatius Press)

Three Philosophies of Life: Ecclesiastes, Job, and Song of Songs (Ignatius Press) (life as vanity, life as suffering, life as love)

Heaven, the Heart's Deepest Longing (Ignatius Press)

Handbook of Christian Apologetics (InterVarsity Press)

Fundamentals of the Faith (Ignatius Press)

Between Heaven and Hell (InterVarsity Press) (C.S. Lewis, Aldous Huxley, and John F. Kennedy in a postmortem debate in the next world about Jesus)

The Best Things in Life (InterVarsity Press) (Socrates appears on the campus of Desperate State University and questions opposite kinds of students, Peter Pragma and Felicia Flake, about values)

The Philosophy of Jesus (St. Augustine's Press)

Jesus-Shock (St. Augustine's Press)

An Ocean Full of Angels (St. Augustine's Press) (a supernatural novel)

Readers interested in finding out what is next not for Socrates but for themselves might try the open-minded experiment of praying. For even if you do not believe in God, God believes in you.